Smithsonian

WE ARE HERE

30 INSPIRING
ASIAN AMERICANS
AND PACIFIC ISLANDERS
WHO HAVE SHAPED
THE UNITED STATES

WRITTEN BY NAOMI HIRAHARA
ILLUSTRATED BY ILLI FERANDEZ

Foreword by Theodore S. Gonzalves
Introduction by Lisa S. Sasaki
Reflection Guide by Andrea Kim Neighbors
and Healoha Johnston

RP|KIDS
PHILADELPHIA

Running Press Kids
Hachette Book Group
1290 Avenue of the Americas, New York, NY 10104
www.runningpress.com/rpkids
@runningpresskids

Printed in Malaysia

First Edition: October 2022

Published by Running Press Kids, an imprint of Perseus Books, LLC,
a subsidiary of Hachette Book Group, Inc. The Running Press Kids name
and logo is a trademark of the Hachette Book Group.

The Hachette Speakers Bureau provides a wide range of authors for speaking events.
To find out more, go to www.hachettespeakersbureau.com or call (866) 376-6591.

The publisher is not responsible for websites (or their content)
that are not owned by the publisher.

Print book cover and interior design by Frances J. Soo Ping Chow.

Library of Congress Cataloging-in-Publication Data Names: Hirahara, Naomi, 1962–
author. | Ferandez, Illi, illustrator. Title: We are here : 30 inspiring Asian Americans and
Pacific Islanders who have shaped the United States / by Naomi Hirahara; illustrated by
Illi Ferandez; foreword by Theodore S. Gonzalves; introduction by Lisa S. Sasaki; reading
guide by Andrea Kim Neighbors and Healoha Johnston. Other titles: 30 inspiring Asian
Americans and Pacific Islanders who have shaped the United States Description:
First edition. | Philadelphia: Running Press Kids, 2022. Identifiers: LCCN 2021049156 |
ISBN 9780762479658 (hardcover) | ISBN 9780762479665 (ebook) Subjects: LCSH: Asian
Americans—Biography—Juvenile literature. | Pacific Islander Americans—Biography—
Juvenile literature. Classification: LCC E184.A75 H567 2022 | DDC 920.0092/95073—
dc23/eng/20211108 LC record available at https://lccn.loc.gov/2021049156

ISBNs: 978-0-7624-7965-8 (hardcover), 978-0-7624-7966-5 (ebook)

PCF

10 9 8 7 6 5 4 3 2

CONTENTS

FOREWORD

by Theodore S. Gonzalves

We are here . . . because you were there. That sentence has become shorthand for a number of experiences—sojourns, migrations, and movements. It can certainly be used to trace that long arc of Asian American and Pacific Islander (AAPI) stories that this book suggests through individual portraits. Who is the "you" in that sentence? Take a look at Loni Ding's fantastic three-part documentary called *Ancestors in the Americas*. The first episode is titled "Coolies, Settlers, and Sailors: Voyage to the New World." It helped to rearrange my thinking about my family's personal journey from the Philippines to the United States. But it did much more. It demonstrated the need for all of us to think more critically about where and when "we" entered this evolving American story. Ding stepped back centuries and widened the frame, making global connections to AAPI routes and roots. These journeys were not just to the United States, but to the Americas as a hemisphere. One of the historians Ding interviewed for the program reminded viewers that Europe had had Asia on its mind for centuries. So much so, an Italian sailor was financed by Spanish funds in the search for an elusive passage to the "Orient." He landed in what's now called the Bahamas and thought he was in the "Indies." And consider how the United States' third president, Thomas Jefferson, commissioned Lewis and Clark's expedition to find an overland path to the Pacific Coast and commerce.

Our stories have been woven into the hemisphere for centuries. With the formal end of the global trade of enslaved Africans in the early 1800s, Indians and Chinese were sent to the Americas as replacement labor. From 1565 to 1815, a grand galleon trade route linked Nagasaki,

Macau, Malacca, and Goa to Lisbon, Seville, Antwerp, Havana, Panama, Rio, and Lima—with everything anchored between Manila and Acapulco. *We've been here.*

The year 2022 marks the Smithsonian Asian Pacific American Center's twenty-fifth year of researching, documenting, and sharing AAPI stories. *We Are Here* is the perfect opportunity to acknowledge the diversity and pace of our communities' growth. Beyond the global cities we've called home—Honolulu, San Francisco, Seattle, Los Angeles, Chicago, and New York City—you're just as likely to find our families and networks in Atlanta, Minneapolis, Little Rock, Houston, and Madison. Numbering more than twenty-four million persons, Asian Americans and Pacific Islanders are the fastest-growing racial group in the country. Of the ten most commonly spoken languages in US homes other than English and Spanish, four hail from Asia. *We're everywhere.*

When the Asian American movement was in full swing, poet-activists like Janice Mirikitani—a Stockton, California–born daughter of farmers—gave us a powerful vision of how to think about the expanse and beauty of our communities. In a poem called "Firepot," she wrote about our routes and roots: ". . . we have been fractured / made to look at each other / as though we are / divided / but if we see with clear eyes, we know we are bound by common shackles:

Manila to Vietnam
Korea to Laos   China to the Islands
Hiroshima to Cambodia   Post St. to Hunters Pt.
Kearney St. to Richmond   Mission to the Valley
Bound by our Survival
Bound by our Strengths . . ."

INTRODUCTION

by Lisa S. Sasaki

We Are Here: 30 Inspiring Asian Americans and Pacific Islanders Who Have Shaped the United States will introduce you to members of diverse communities and their stories of resilience, adversity, and joy. It is my honor to be a part of a book that will reach readers like you across the United States, sharing stories that I have been proud to learn more about as director of the Smithsonian Asian Pacific American Center. These stories make our work at the Smithsonian stronger and more inclusive. They also reflect fuller American stories that all readers deserve to see.

This book came together during a difficult time for our communities. The global spread of COVID-19 led to incidents of hate and bias against Asian American elders, women, and young adults. These heartbreaking incidents prompted the center and the Smithsonian to think about how we could better support our communities and the nation. We created a virtual care package, filled with meditations, short films, and musical performances created by Asian Americans and Pacific Islanders. We also developed new resources for teachers and caregivers about the impacts of negative stereotypes on AAPI communities and how to unlearn these biases. Sadly, these incidents are not new but part of a longer American history that we don't often learn about in school.

It is my hope that these thirty profiles of incredible AAPIs introduce you to stories that you did not know before. I also hope these profiles spark conversations with your family, friends, and classmates about why AAPI stories are important to learn. As you read the following pages, you may be surprised by who you see in this book. Because we value inclusion and solidarity, you'll read the stories of Pacific Islanders and

Arab Americans. Their experiences have not always been visible in AAPI accounts, yet Pacific Islander, Arab American, and Persian American experiences are deeply intertwined and representative of AAPI communities and identities. We selected thirty profiles that speak to our global connections and histories, but they are not reflective of all AAPI stories. There are 22 million Asian Americans and 1.5 million Native Hawaiians and Pacific Islanders in the United States. In Hawai'i alone, 700,000 Native Hawaiians and Pacific Islanders live there today. While you'll meet inspiring activists, artists, musicians, actors, writers, scientists, and entrepreneurs, this is just a start. There are many more stories to tell.

We thank our colleagues at Hachette Group/Running Press Kids and Smithsonian Enterprises for telling these stories with the Asian Pacific American Center. We thank Jill Corcoran at Smithsonian Enterprises and Allison Cohen at Running Press for believing in our vision for this book. Special thanks to our colleague Sojin Kim at the Smithsonian Center for Folklife and Cultural Heritage. Finally, acknowledgment must also go to the center's staff for their many contributions and leadership on this project: Theodore S. Gonzalves, Andrea Kim Neighbors, Healoha Johnston, Lawrence-Minh Bùi Davis, Kālewa Correa, Adriel Luis, Nafisa Isa, Wendy Kennedy, Marynissa Pedroza, Catherine Lee, and Mary Woodward.

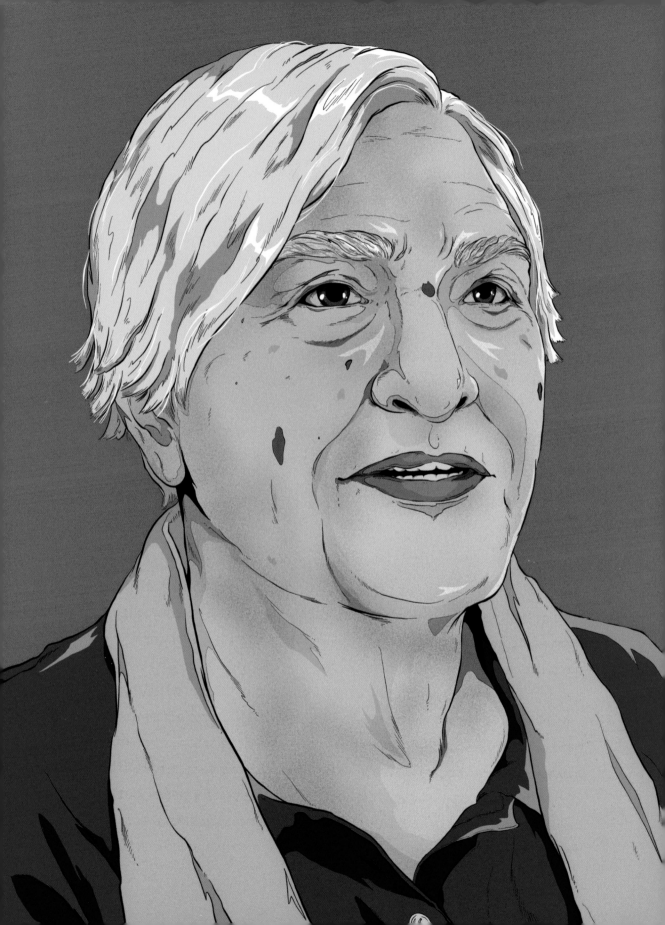

Etel Adnan

(1925–2021)

Learning to communicate in different languages was part of Etel Adnan's childhood in her birthplace of Beirut, the capital of a newly created Lebanon. Her father was a Syrian Muslim and her mother a Greek Christian. After World War I, French and British military powers colonized regions in Southwest Asia and North Africa and forcefully redefined long-standing government structures under their nation-states. Etel grew up speaking Greek and Turkish at home, French at a Catholic convent school, and Arabic on the street.

*For me, [painting] was
a new language, a new world.*

Etel was interested in becoming an engineer or architect, but she was discouraged from doing so because she was a girl. While Etel was in school in Beirut, a centuries-old city known as an intellectual and cultural hub, a teacher introduced her to many important French poets, and she began writing poems about the sun and sea in French. She studied philosophy at the University of Paris and stayed in France until the early years of the Algerian War of Independence. In 1955 Etel, dismayed with France's treatment of the colonized people in North Africa, left Europe to study at the University of California at Berkeley and at Harvard. "I didn't want to read French or write it; it was like a boycott, a rejection," said Etel.

While teaching at a small Catholic college in Northern California, Etel adopted a new language: painting. She applied paint directly from the tube on a canvas and created squares of color with a palette knife. Etel then moved from exclusively abstract forms to working with accordion-folded sketchbooks in which she mixed drawings with writing and poetry. Tapestries integrated with colors from the Persian rugs of her youth also became part of her signature work. Inspired by poets protesting the Vietnam War, she returned to writing and published a collection of poems, *Moonshots*, in English in 1966. In the 1970s she moved to an area north of San Francisco marked by a majestic peak, Mount Tamalpais, inspiring a series of creative works, both visual and written.

In 1977 she wrote a novel, *Sitt Marie Rose*, based on a true story of a Lebanese woman kidnapped by soldiers during the civil war in Lebanon. A heralded representation of war literature, the novel has been translated into ten languages. In her writings, Adnan questioned how power and oppression exist in social situations. She often considered gender roles as well as political dynamics between Indigenous, displaced, and settler groups to share stories about human migration, liberation, and borders.

Etel's paintings have been acquired and displayed in museums across the world. She published many books in English and French, wrote plays, and made movies. In the same way that her life spanned multiple countries, the products of her artistic expression knew no boundaries.

Eddie Aikau

(1946–1978)

Eddie Aikau, the first lifeguard at Waimea Bay on the island of Oʻahu in Hawaiʻi, dedicated his life to helping others. The third of six children, Eddie first surfed the waves of Hawaiʻi on a wooden board called a paipo, as his Hawaiian ancestors did. Since the illegal overthrow of the Hawaiian kingdom by agents backed by the US military in 1893, Native Hawaiian people have been alienated within their own homelands. The water was a place of freedom for Eddie.

Walls Beach, a popular spot for local families in Waikīkī, was where Eddie formed a relationship with the waves on his paipo and then foam and resin surfboards of the 1960s. By age seventeen, he was one of the top surfers in Hawaiʻi. The more challenging waves, however, were on the North Shore of Oʻahu, an area taken over by non-Hawaiian surfers.

In 1965 a surf championship, named in honor of the father of modern surfing, Duke Kahanamoku, was established on the North Shore. It was an invitational, and Eddie was eager to compete. Despite his talent, he wasn't invited—in fact, hardly any Native Hawaiians were. Most of the surfers were non-Hawaiian, and many of them were from outside of Hawaiʻi. This was a bitter reminder that while surfing had been developed by Native Hawaiians, discriminatory practices excluded them from the sports of their ancestors.

Eddie didn't give up. He was invited the following year and finished sixth. One day forty-foot waves hit the North Shore, and Eddie surfed them. These giant swells soon attracted surfers of various skill levels across the globe. Some were overwhelmed by the dangerous conditions at Waimea Bay and drowned. Honolulu mayor Frank Fasi sent out a call for an experienced waterman to watch over the surfers, and in 1967 Eddie accepted his new role on the North Shore as a lifeguard. Out of five hundred rescues over eleven years, he did not lose a single swimmer or surfer.

I did it for all the Hawaiians.

In 1972 Eddie was selected to represent the United States with two white men in a surf competition in South Africa, which was under apartheid. Away from his home for the first time, he was prevented from checking into a whites-only hotel. Fortunately, Eddie was aided by sympathetic white South Africans, who made sure that he had a safe place to stay. Eddie was eliminated on the second day of the three-day contest and spent the rest of the ten-day trip surfing with new friends in South Africa's legendary surf break, Jeffreys Bay.

Returning to Hawai'i, Eddie had a new challenge to overcome. Until this point, winning "The Duke" competition had been out of Eddie's reach. His younger brother, Clyde, won in 1973. Finally, in December 1977, Eddie captured the championship at the age of thirty-one. "I did it for all the Hawaiians," he said.

Eddie Aikau was a member of the original crew aboard the *Hōkūle'a*, a double-hulled canoe built according to the ancestral technology of Pacific Islanders who traveled great distances between islands across

Oceania. Guided by their expertise, using the stars as a map, and closely observing the atmospheric and oceanic conditions, the crew of the *Hōkūleʻa* successfully landed in Tahiti from Hawaiʻi in 1976. Two years later, the *Hōkūleʻa* would set sail again, and Eddie would be on it. The voyage to Tahiti was tumultuous, and the *Hōkūleʻa* capsized. Concerned for the lives of their fellow travelers, it was decided that Eddie would paddle out with his surfboard to get help on land. He was lost at sea, while the rest of the crew members were rescued the next day. Despite days of searching by authorities—the largest air-sea search in Hawaiian history—his body was never found.

To honor his memory, a surf competition called "The Eddie" was started in 1984.

Grace Lee Boggs

(1915–2015)

Grace Lee Boggs was born above her father's Chinese restaurant in downtown Providence, Rhode Island. She was the fourth of six children born to her Chinese immigrant father and his second wife. Her Chinese name was Yu Ping, meaning "Jade Peace." Her English name, Grace, was given to her by the missionary who taught her father English.

Grace's family later moved from Providence to New York City, where her father opened two large restaurants on Broadway. Although the Lees were financially stable, living in a white middle-class neighborhood in Jackson Heights, they still encountered prejudice. Restrictive covenants barred the sale of property to persons of Chinese heritage, so the deed to the family house had to be in the name of an Irish contractor.

In the neighborhood, Grace was often asked about her nationality.

"American," she'd patiently reply.

Grace, who was a thinker and intellectual since girlhood, enrolled at age sixteen in Barnard College, a private women's school in New York City. She was one of only three students of color on the campus. By her junior year, Grace lost interest in her general education classes. Instead, she became obsessed with philosophy. "All I knew was that I was feeling the need to think for myself," she wrote in her biography.

After graduating with a bachelor's degree in philosophy, Grace looked for a job. Many companies rejected her, saying, "We don't hire Orientals."

Grace pursued higher education and was accepted into a graduate philosophy program at Bryn Mawr College in Pennsylvania. In the fall of 1940, Grace moved to Chicago, a city that seemed to offer a new American promise. She found work in the philosophy library of the University of Chicago for ten dollars a week, an amount so low that she had to find free housing in a rat-infested basement. The poor housing conditions led Grace to connect with a tenants-rights organization, through which she became more aware of the struggles of the Black community. Black people from the Deep South had migrated to cities like Chicago, during a movement known as the Great Migration, but could not find work in the defense industry during World War II due to racial discrimination. Protesters mobilized throughout the nation,

We have to change ourselves in order to change the world.

resulting in a presidential order to bar such bias. Watching the progress of this movement, Grace knew that she wanted to commit her life to becoming an activist.

Her quest took her to New York and finally Detroit, where she helped to edit the radical newsletter *Correspondence*. Here Grace met a Chrysler autoworker and Alabama-born Black activist, James Boggs. The couple married in 1953. They were a powerful literary duo with razor-sharp minds committed to making the United States a better place for all.

Grace was constantly evolving and changing. While active in the Black Power movement in Detroit in the 1960s, she began to rethink the role of nonviolent protest after the city's 1967 rebellion. While the 1967 Detroit Riots were instigated by a police raid on an after-hours nightclub, the event reflected a larger trend of racial inequality and police brutality against Black communities that characterized US urban centers during the 1960s. These events prompted Grace to reflect that nonviolence was an important philosophy because it "respects the capacity for human beings to grow their souls."

After her husband's death in 1993, Grace again made changes in her life. To reach a new activist generation eager to receive her wisdom, she wrote an autobiography, *Living for Change,* and was featured in the documentary *American Revolutionary: The Evolution of Grace Lee Boggs.* While Detroit grappled with the decline of the auto industry due to automation, Grace saw opportunity. Through Detroit Summer, a youth program she cofounded, volunteers turned vacant lots into community gardens and painted colorful murals on walls of abandoned buildings. "I think of gardens as the basis of hope," she said.

Lydia X. Z. Brown

(1993–)

Each one of us is obligated to use whatever resources we have to fight and challenge oppression in all of its forms.

Lydia X. Z. Brown, born in Suzhou, a city just west of Shanghai, China, was adopted at age one by a US family and taken to live in Melrose, a predominantly white town in the Greater Boston area.

A creative writer from a young age, Lydia was identified as autistic in the eighth grade and was told to keep silent about the diagnosis. The message they received was that having autism meant something was wrong or broken with them.

During high school Lydia participated in an autism awareness walk sponsored by a nonprofit organization. After successfully raising more than $1,200 from various pledges, Lydia learned that the organization was not fulfilling its stated mission. Instead of returning the money to donors and confronting the organization, Lydia went a step further by reaching out to the group of people who had publicized the nonprofit organization's misconduct to learn more about their work.

This led Lydia to become involved with the Boston chapter of the Autistic Self Advocacy Network (ASAN), one of the largest policy-focused disability-rights organizations run by autistic people. "For them, being autistic was not a defect, it wasn't something that needed to be fixed or cured, but it was the way their brain worked. It was disabling to be sure, but it wasn't an inherent problem," stated Lydia.

In the eleventh grade, Lydia's advocacy continued. They worked with a Massachusetts state senator to introduce a law that would require that the state police be trained to interact with people with autism and other disabilities.

After high school, Lydia took their biggest personal risk, coming out as nonbinary and genderqueer in a community that was not particularly welcoming of those identities.

Lydia pursued a degree in Arabic from Georgetown University. They quickly found themselves pulled into advocacy for disabled people. For example, when a nine-year-old autistic boy from Kentucky was stuffed into an occupational therapy bag and left in the school hallway as disciplinary action by an untrained teacher, Lydia began circulating a petition demanding policy change. More than two hundred thousand people signed the petition, sparking discussion about the treatment of autistic students. Lydia also served as the school's first undersecretary of disability affairs for the Georgetown University Student Association and cofounded the Washington Metro Disabled Students Collective. By senior year, they also became a policy analyst with ASAN's national office in Washington, DC. During Lydia's undergraduate career, they also launched their popular blog, *Autistic Hoya* ("Hoya" referring to the campus's nickname), which explores disability justice and the intersectionality of race and queer/trans rights.

Lydia's work and advocacy did not go unnoticed. In 2013 Lydia was one of eight disability-rights advocates President Barack Obama honored at the "White House Champions of Change: 23rd Anniversary of the Americans with Disabilities" event.

Instead of pursuing a doctorate in Arabic studies, Lydia felt pulled toward disability justice and subsequently earned a law degree from Northeastern University that helped them gain the necessary tools to reduce or stop forms of violence targeted toward autistic people by the global majority. Now Lydia continues to teach as an attorney and organizer as well as fight for reparations for disabled people.

Momi Cazimero

(1933–)

Momi Cazimero grew up the oldest of five children on Hawai'i Island. Surrounded by cane fields, she was raised by her maternal grandparents, who showed love and support through action. Her beloved grandfather told her, "If you like, you can." If Momi committed herself to a goal, she could achieve it.

When Momi was eight years old, her grandfather died, thrusting her into a dark period of her life. She had to return to a difficult relationship with her father in an already crowded home.

In the fourth grade, a teacher gave the class an assignment to describe a unique and unusual object. On the way to Japanese-language school, Momi spied an upside-down hibiscus on a hedge. She drew it, wrote an accompanying essay, and included a cover on her assignment. When she turned it in, the teacher told her she was a very good artist.

Momi was shocked. That was the first time anyone told her she was good at anything.

"What you did was that you didn't give me the minimum; you gave me something more than I asked," the teacher said. Momi kept those words close to her heart.

When Momi was eleven, she was accepted into Kamehameha School on the nearby island of O'ahu. Kamehameha's admissions policy favored

students of Native Hawaiian ancestry, and since her mother was of both Native Hawaiian and Scottish heritage, she qualified. Momi lived in the school dormitory during the term and in her aunt's house during the summer.

At Kamehameha, students bullied Momi. She would sit on the edge of her bed and try to invoke her dead grandfather's presence. "Okay, Grandpa, I'm waiting for you." He never came, and Momi realized she would have to overcome problems on her own.

She graduated from high school and attended the University of Hawai'i at Mānoa with the intention of becoming an art teacher. At the university, she met Kenneth Kingery, a design professor who would become one of her mentors. Momi was assigned to work on the college yearbook, a coveted position. In a meeting, the printer publicly insulted her. When Professor Kingery heard what had happened, he marched into the print shop with Momi and confronted the owner and staff, saying that they had demeaned the profession and themselves. "She will one day amount to more than you will ever be," he declared. After this disturbing encounter, Momi learned that she would always be decisive and never tolerate abuse from anyone.

After graduating with a bachelor's degree in fine arts, Momi got a job with a commercial artist. Her ambition, however, was to someday be her own boss and open her own business. Despite the discrimination she experienced in a male-dominated field, in 1972 she founded the first woman-owned graphic design firm in Hawai'i, Graphic House.

"There was enough of a competitive spirit about me that sometimes I wanted to do it just because someone said I couldn't," she said.

Once she found a location for her business in Honolulu, her father came to the property. He got down on his hands and knees and scrubbed the entire floor. Momi understood this action to mean that he was sorry for mistreating and underestimating her in the past.

In terms of her design aesthetic, Momi incorporated Hawaiian iconography whenever appropriate. "When you're designing a logo, you must get to its essence," she said.

I thrived on competition.

With her deliberate and precise approach, Momi attracted a growing number of clients, eventually landing accounts with the largest Hawai'i-based companies. She also served on the University of Hawai'i Board of Regents and Hawai'i's Judicial Selection Commission. "I wanted to be certain that I paved the way for other women to follow. I really considered that a responsibility."

Manny Crisostomo

(1958–)

Manny Crisostomo was an intern reporter at the *Pacific Daily News (PDN)*, a newspaper on the island of Guam, known by its people as Guåhan, when he discovered that the best way for him to document stories was through photography. With a camera that his mother had purchased for him, Manny was ready to go where his curiosity took him.

After three years at the university and working in the photo lab at the *PDN*, Manny left his home island for the University of Missouri and its renowned journalism department. He graduated with a bachelor's degree in journalism in 1982.

After graduation he joined the *Detroit Free Press*, a daily newspaper. His ability to capture stirring photographs, full of emotion and intimacy, was quickly recognized by various news organizations. During a two-year period, he worked on two intense series: "Youth Outlaws," which followed young people in juvenile detention, and "Too Young to Die," a special report on guns, crack addiction, and violence among Detroit teens. Both projects made him curious about the real lives of high school students.

He wrote a letter to the superintendent of Detroit Public Schools to see if he could devote an entire year to documenting life at school. He was granted permission, resulting in "A Class Act: The Life and Times of Southwestern High School." Published in the *Detroit Free Press* in June 1988, the special section featured more than sixty photos of students experiencing the highs and lows of life, a mirror of the Detroit community at large. During this time, Manny became friends with the people he interviewed, feeling especially empathetic toward those "teetering on the edge that have the potential to warm our hearts or to break our hearts. They are, after all, our children."

Being open to spirit, the universe.

In the early 1980s, Manny had already been nominated three times for the Pulitzer Prize, the highest honor in journalism. His documentation of Southwestern High School earned him the honor in feature photography in 1989. This was the first time for a CHamoru, an Indigenous person of Micronesia, to win a Pulitzer. During the same year, Manny received an honorary doctorate degree from the University of Guam.

Two years later, he took a sabbatical from the newspaper and returned to his home island to teach and chronicle the beauty of both the people and the landscape. He hand-painted a canvas backdrop, which he took with him to various cultural gatherings, to do on-location portraits. Those photographs formed the coffee-table book *Legacy of Guam: I Kustumbren Chamoru.*

In 1995 he began publishing *Latte Magazine*, a publication celebrating life in Micronesia, and opened up a gallery to feature the region's artists.

After these endeavors in Guåhan, he moved to California, taught photojournalism at colleges, and worked at the *Sacramento Bee* as a

multimedia editor and senior photographer. He traveled to war zones in Africa to document children orphaned in the long Eritrea-Ethiopia conflict and follow Hmong refugees as they traveled from camps in Thailand to the United States. He also diversified into video to capture the plight of childhood obesity in a series called "The Weight," which garnered him multiple awards.

Manny advises future photographers to "get out there and take pictures. Shoot a lot, but with a personal approach to your subject— with objectivity, compassion, and sensitivity—you get a picture of significance."

Taimane Gardner

(1989–)

When Hawaiʻi-born Taimane Gardner was five, her father gave her an ʻukulele, a popular four-stringed instrument that was invented in Hawaiʻi and modeled after string instruments introduced by Portuguese immigrants. From a young age, Taimane, who already loved to perform and dance like her mother, a former Miss Sāmoa and flight attendant, used the ʻukulele to produce transcendent music, incorporating influences from different times and places.

At the age of seven, Taimane began performing cover songs, including her father's favorite rock songs from the 1970s, on the streets of Waikīkī. With her father watching over her, Taimane managed to draw a crowd, including a group of boys who joined in with bongos and other instruments. Soon they would be regularly busking on Friday evenings in front of the Pacific Beach Hotel.

One evening a Hawaiʻi musical icon, Don Ho, stopped by to watch. He was mesmerized by the young Taimane and asked her to join his show in a Waikīkī hotel. Taimane got her first job at age thirteen.

She would play one or two songs at the beginning of the show only once a week. That grew to two to three nights a week. "Uncle" Don, whose "Tiny Bubbles" song hit the *Billboard* charts in the 1960s, never

gave Taimane any musical advice. But she was able to learn from the consummate entertainer how to run a show and connect with the audience. She continued to perform with Don for five years until his death.

She continued to hone her craft as a performer in Honolulu's Chinatown, where eclectic audiences in art houses embraced her unusual mashups and love for a wide array of genres, from flamenco to classical music.

With exposure to so many different music and ʻukulele masters, Taimane, who plays by ear, has been introduced to many styles and gravitates toward melodies that are new to her.

Taimane sometimes practiced blindfolded, training herself to not

---

ʻUkulele, although underestimated, can definitely blow some minds.

---

look at the strings of her ʻukulele so that she could instead direct her attention to the faces of audience members.

After her beloved mother died when Taimane was in her twenties, the ʻukulele player made a pilgrimage to her roots in Sāmoa, which has influenced her original compositions. She also sings and will sometimes vocalize, using sounds rather than words in her performances. Harking back to her childhood passion, she's written songs inspired by each of the planets and elements.

Her nimble finger work and ferocious energy have captured music producers and event bookers. While her active YouTube channel has attracted millions of viewers, she has also performed at venues like South by Southwest and been featured on National Public Radio's *Tiny Desk Concerts*.

Calvin and Charlene Hoe

(Calvin: 1945–) (Charlene: 1946–)

Calvin Hoe was born at home in Hakipu'u, facing Kāne'ohe Bay on Hawai'i's island of O'ahu. The name Hakipu'u means "Broken Hill" in Hawaiian, referring to the jagged mountains surrounding the green, fertile valley.

When Calvin was a child, the land of his maternal family flooded. His parents called city public works, and the river was dredged.

Years later, when Calvin was in his twenties, joined by his wife, Charlene, he returned to the Hakipu'u area. Originally from South Dakota, Charlene, a non-Hawaiian woman, met Calvin while she was attending Macalester College in Minnesota. Together, they served in the Peace Corps where they spent a year living on Lukonor in Chuuk and another on Saipan in the Northern Mariana Islands. They were hoping to grow lo'i kalo, wetland taro, a nonglutenous root vegetable that is central to the Native Hawaiian diet, origin story, and culture when they returned to Hakipu'u. Nutritious and with high fiber, kalo is used to make poi, a staple in the Polynesian diet. Calvin and Charlene were able to purchase a remnant of his past—a small century-old poi factory operated by a Japanese American family in Waiāhole.

One day the springs that provided water to the region dried up. "I've never seen that in my whole life," said Calvin.

He remembered the time of the flood during his boyhood years, when his parents went to the city for help. So he did the same.

"Eh, there's no water. What can we do?" he asked city officials.

"You have to go to the state, the Department of Land and Natural Resources."

After he approached them, officials told Calvin that was not their kuleana, or responsibility. "You have to go to the federal people."

Calvin obliged and approached the US Army Corps of Engineers. "Our stream is dry," he said.

"We only handle navigable water," the Corps of Engineers told him. In other words, if the waterways were not deep enough for a ship to pass through, the federal government was not responsible for fixing the problem.

Who was going to take care of this? Calvin thought about it and came to the conclusion: us—we can take care of this.

As part of their investigation to understand what was happening, he and Charlene, with their children in tow, went from island to island within Hawaiʻi to understand the cause of this problem. The sugar plantations diverted water in Hawaiʻi during the late 1800s to early 1900s for their exploitative and unsustainable business enterprises. In the 1970s, development in the more populated parts of Oʻahu was leaving springs like the one in Hakipuʻu dry. The solution, they determined, was to limit unsustainable forms of development on the island.

As a result of their work, Charlene became one of 102 delegates to the landmark 1978 Constitutional Convention, which, among its many achievements, created a provision in the state constitution calling for the protection of Hawaiʻi's natural resources.

To help preserve Native Hawaiian culture, Calvin and Charlene developed a grassroots approach. They turned the poi factory in Waiāhole into an art gallery to celebrate Pacific arts during the 1980s,

We can take care of this.

and later evolved the space into a rentable kitchen for people to experiment with food and agricultural production ideas.

They cofounded Hakipuʻu Academy, a Hawaiian knowledge- and project-based public charter school. In addition to advocacy and environmental policy work, Charlene spent much of her career as an educator at Kamehameha Schools, first as an art teacher and then as a lead member of the organization's strategic planning teams. This work prepared her to undertake the administration of the Hakipuʻu Learning Center established first as a multigenerational, lifelong place of learning and then became the Academy. Calvin devoted more time to making and playing Native Hawaiian pre-continual contact instruments and teaching these practices to students. Instruments include the ʻohe hano ihu, or bamboo nose flute, and hōkiokio, other flutes made from gourds, kamani nuts, and coconuts.

Calvin's craftsmanship has been recognized by institutions such as the Smithsonian, which has invited him multiple times to participate in cultural events and performances. These workshops center not only on the creation of these ancient instruments, but also on the storytelling that accompanies the music. In this way, Calvin has served as an important kūpuna, or elder, to share Indigenous knowledge with younger generations.

The poi factory has since been transformed into a seller of nutritious plate lunches with foods that make up a classical Hawaiian diet and various dishes created with local ingredients. Regularly selling out is poi, hand pounded by Calvin and Charlene's son, Liko, from kalo grown in the region's valley.

Schuyler Miwon Hong Bailar

(1996–)

I'm just presenting the truest part of myself.

Schuyler Miwon Hong Bailar had been a water baby from the age of one and by high school was one of the top breaststrokers among female competitors in the nation. An acceptance to Harvard and its women's swim team followed. But Schuyler wasn't happy. A mountain-bike accident led to depression, an eating disorder, and time to think deeply at an inpatient facility. The truth emerged.

"Dad, I think I'm transgender," Schuyler said, crying. Schuyler had always feared developing breasts and, for an elementary school art assignment calling for students to imagine themselves as old people, Schuyler drew a white-haired man with a mustache.

With full parental support, Schuyler began to transition to presenting as male before starting college. He feared most coming out to his conservative Catholic Korean immigrant grandmother, his mother's mother. He surprisingly received her acceptance. As Korean women have traditionally served as caregivers for aging parents, she was most concerned about whether her daughter and son-in-law, now without a daughter themselves, would be looked after in their old age. Schuyler not only pledged his support, but also got a tattoo in his grandmother's Korean handwriting, "Take care of your parents," near his heart and next to the scar of his top surgery.

As he took steps to come out, a primary question lingered: What would happen to his first love, swimming? Being underwater made him feel calm and quiet inside. At great risk to losing his sport while confirming his identity, he informed his college coach about his decision to transition and eventually undergo surgery to remove his breasts.

Based on NCAA rules, Schuyler could still compete in the female category in the water while being a man outside the pool—as long as he did not undergo testosterone hormone treatment. But the women's coach wondered if that was the best option. College was a time for reinvention, not for leading a double life. The coach consulted with the coach of the men's swim team. He went to his team to ask the members if any of them objected to Schuyler joining them in the next season. No one did.

As a member of the men's swim team, Schuyler became the first openly transgender college student to compete in a Division I sport. When he graduated in 2019 with a bachelor's degree in cognitive neuroscience and evolutionary psychology, Schuyler was ranked in the top 15 percent in the NCAA in men's breaststroke.

Active on social media (@pinkmantary) and a frequent guest on television news programs, he is now a life coach, inspirational speaker, and equity advocate and consultant. He is committed to sharing his story to educate the public and inspire young people. In 2021 he published his first novel about a tween swimmer who loves being in the water and also happens to be transgender, titled *Obie Is Man Enough*.

Dinah Jane

(1997–)

Singer Dinah Jane, formerly of the pop girl group Fifth Harmony, was born Dinah Jane Hansen in Santa Ana, California. From a large Pacific Islander family, she grew up in her grandparents' four-bedroom house that she shared with her parents, siblings, uncles, aunt, and cousins. At one time, twenty-three people lived under one roof.

Being the oldest of eight children and the oldest of eighteen grandchildren, Dinah Jane was viewed as the "face" of the family. As a result, she was used to dealing with the pressure of being the firstborn. With so many young cousins underfoot, Dinah never felt alone at home. Music permeated the home, with Dinah's father playing reggae CDs and her mother singing at the Mormon church. Often harmonizing together, the grandchildren would produce variety shows to perform for the grandparents, who would follow the Tongan practice of distributing fakapale, or dollar bills, to express appreciation to entertainers.

Dinah, who began singing when she was four, made her YouTube debut at age eleven when her cousin uploaded a video with the subtitle "Tongan Girl Singing." While Dinah was raised Tongan, she is also of Sāmoan, Fijian, and Danish descent. When Dinah was fifteen years old, she was invited to compete in the Rhode Island round of the television show *The X Factor*. An *American Idol* fan, she respected judge Simon Cowell's opinion. He was also a judge for *The X Factor*, alongside Dinah's idols, Britney Spears and Demi Lovato. After she finished her audition, the audience erupted in applause and cheers.

Dinah, who studied musical theater at the Orange County School of the Arts, was teamed with four other young female performers to form Fifth Harmony in 2012. For the next six years, the group would release best-selling albums that consistently reached the top ten on the *Billboard* charts. Dinah said that being part of a group helped her "to break out of my shell. I was so shy." The other girls would talk over each other, forcing Dinah to break in at times. Her mother encouraged her to speak out, saying, "Closed mouths don't get fed."

It's OK to be vulnerable. That's what makes us stronger.... It makes us braver.

The 2017 announcement that she would perform the Tongan national anthem at the Rugby League World Cup semifinal in New Zealand, known by its people as Aotearoa, generated debate on social media. Some critics argued a group would have been better, as the anthem is never sung by a single person. But as Dinah belted out the anthem, all the Tongan players and fans joined in, their fists over their hearts.

Fifth Harmony went through changes, and, in 2018, Dinah and the three remaining members decided to take an indefinite hiatus and explore what each could do as a solo act. Dinah was the first to release a single, the R&B-influenced pop song "Bottle Up." In 2019 she released a

three-song bundle, "Dinah Jane 1," in which she revealed the complexity of family relations. One of the songs, "Fix It," references how silence can stymie healthy interactions and instructs, "Stand up for yourself."

Dinah's first solo world tour in 2020 was canceled due to the coronavirus pandemic. Although disappointed, Dinah persevered and managed to release a midpandemic single, "Missed a Spot," a fun tropical song that samples the Australian group Men at Work's "Down Under." She also spent time with her family in Orange County, enjoying making brownies with one of her sisters and recording Instagram Lives and TikToks with her relatives.

Kathy Jetñil-Kijiner

(1987–)

Kathy Jetñil-Kijiner was born in the Marshall Islands, a nation of twenty-nine low-lying Micronesian volcanic islands and coral atolls in the central Pacific Ocean between Hawai'i and the Philippines. From 1946 to 1958, the US government conducted nuclear weapons tests on the islands, destroying three islands and leaving radioactivity particles that caused birth defects. Climate change has also wreaked havoc on the islands, leading to droughts, coastal erosion, and rising sea levels that threaten to completely flood the land.

In the 1990s, Kathy's family left the capital city of Majuro for Hawai'i. Kathy, who attended elementary and secondary schools in downtown Honolulu, started writing poetry in the third grade. Her first poem was about an invisible elephant. She did not take poetry seriously until two substitute teachers took over her English class during her senior year of high school. They were spoken-word artists, and their style, perhaps reminiscent of the oral tradition of the Marshall Islands, resonated with Kathy.

Kathy's passion for poetry, performance art, and journalism blossomed at Mills College, in Oakland, California, where she majored in English with an emphasis on creative writing. She returned to the Marshall Islands for two years before returning to Hawai'i to get her

master of arts degree in Pacific Islands studies from her mother's alma mater. She later moved back to the Marshall Islands again and worked at the college at Majuro.

While at home, Kathy wrote poems that shed light on nuclear weapons testing in the Marshall Islands and discrimination against Micronesian people in Hawaiʻi. She answered a call for poets from Micronesia to present at the 2012 Poetry Parnassus, the largest poetry festival ever staged in the United Kingdom, to coincide with the London Olympics. She shared the international stage with Nobel Prize winners and well-established poets.

Words are power.

As climate-change issues grew more pressing, in 2014 Kathy and her cousin founded Jo-Jikum, a Majuro-based nonprofit devoted to educational training programs related to the environment. The same year, Kathy went to New York City to address 120 heads of state at the United Nations Secretary-General's Climate Summit. Selected from 544 candidates, Kathy performed the poem "Dear Matafele Peinem," written to her six-month-old daughter. The power of the moment overwhelmed the heads of state, who gave Kathy and her family a standing ovation.

That poem and many others are featured in Kathy's *Iep Jāltok: Poems from a Marshallese Daughter*, the first published poetry collection by a person from the Marshall Islands. She dedicated her book to her mother, Hilda, who became the first woman to be elected president of the Marshall Islands in 2016. Hilda was also the first woman to serve as head of state in any of the five Micronesian countries of the North Pacific.

As a member of 350 Pacific Climate Warriors, Kathy continues to integrate video and other collaborative partnerships to produce relevant and multilayered work. In 2017 she traveled to Hiroshima Peace Park in Japan to videotape a reading of her poem "Monster," which explores motherhood and the nuclear fallout faced by Marshallese pregnant women. The poem was later adapted into a performance piece, "She Who Dies to Live," at the Smithsonian Asian Pacific American Center's Culture Lab (a pop-up museum experience) 'Ae Kai, in Hawai'i, in 2017.

Despite the challenges that the Marshall Islands face, Kathy remains hopeful and inspired by the young people dedicated to reversing the impacts of climate change. She told a reporter, "For me, I'm just going to continue to fight as long as we're there."

Dwayne "The Rock" Johnson

(1972–)

Hawai'i-born Dwayne was part of a professional wrestling legacy on both sides of his family. His maternal grandfather, High Chief Peter Fanene Leifi Maivia, was descended from a royal family and leader of the clan in Sāmoa. Chief Peter left Sāmoa for Aotearoa/New Zealand, where he trained to become a wrestler. He met his future wife, Ofelia Fuataga Maivia, and they eventually moved to Hawai'i, where their daughter, Dwayne's mother, Ata, was born. Ata eventually married Rocky Johnson, a Black Canadian wrestler who occasionally tag-teamed Chief Peter in the ring.

Being the son of a pro wrestler was difficult. Income was unstable, and the family had to move several times to be part of the professional wrestling circuit. Dwayne had to learn how to make friends quickly and be on his own. When his role model, Chief Peter, whose body was adorned with tattoos, died of cancer when Dwayne was ten, he went into a tailspin. He got into fights and was arrested for petty crimes.

Dwayne turned to the gym to deal with his pain and fears. He finally found stability when a high school coach recruited him to play football when the family moved to Bethlehem, Pennsylvania. Although Dwayne was relatively new to the game, he had the size and natural physical ability to excel in the sport. He became so skilled that the top-rated University of Miami offered him a full scholarship to play football. Dwayne thought he was on his way to the National Football League and good money.

Dwayne graduated in 1995 with a bachelor's degree in criminology and physiology but wasn't drafted by the NFL. He was offered a spot as a linebacker with a team in the Canadian Football League but was cut after only two months. He returned to live with his parents in Tampa, Florida, with only seven dollars in his pocket.

*Stay strong, have faith,
and keep pushing through.*

Against his father's wishes, Dwayne decided to follow in his family's footsteps and become a professional wrestler. He observed that connecting with the audience was an important quality. Dwayne wrestled under the name Rocky Maivia, but found true success when he reinvented himself as a charming villain named the Rock.

Acting was his next step, and he rose to become the highest-paid actor in the world, playing recurring lead roles in popular movie franchises. He also formed his own production company, which he named Seven Buck Productions in memory of the down-and-out situation in which he found himself at one point in his life.

Dwayne was even able to showcase his Sāmoan heritage in a spin-off to *The Fast and the Furious* franchise, *Hobbs & Shaw*. He played Luke Hobbs, who returns to his childhood Sāmoa in the climactic ending, in

which Sāmoan warriors overwhelm villains seeking to poison the world with a supervirus. The actor also joined the kiʻaʻi, or guardians, protecting Maunakea, Hawaiʻi's highest point and considered sacred ground, from the installation of a giant telescope.

On Christmas 2018, Dwayne surprised his mother with a gift—a new house anywhere in the United States, signaling that the family's financial insecurities were a thing of the past.

Channapha Khamvongsa

(1973–)

During the Vietnam War, Laos sustained two million tons of bombs—more than the combined number of bombs dropped on Germany and Japan during World War II. Many of these explosives, some the size of a tennis ball, did not detonate at that time. Decades later, they are tragically responsible for maiming and killing innocent farmers and children in this Southeast Asian country. These "bombies"—small bombs released in clusters that the United States dropped from the mid-1960s to 1970s—were part of the secret war in Laos, largely unknown to people in the United States.

*Bring something positive
from something so dark.*

Channapha Khamvongsa, born in Laos before coming to the United States as a refugee, was only six years old when she and her family settled in the state of Virginia. Her parents wanted her and her siblings to look toward the future and live a happy life. Channapha liked to help people and, in middle school, volunteered with the Red Cross to provide

underprivileged children with toys. In time, through conversations with family elders and community members, Channapha learned the legacy of the bombings in Laos and understood the extent of the damage her country of birth had suffered.

Empowered with this knowledge, Channapha graduated from high school and pursued an education in public service, earning her bachelor's degree in public administration from George Mason University and her master's in public policy from Georgetown University. She subsequently worked for philanthropic foundations, such as the Ford Foundation and NEO Philanthropy on issues such as immigrant rights and leadership. Still, the plight of her people remained at the top of her mind.

In 2004 Channapha founded Legacies of War, a nonprofit organization focused on raising awareness about the undetonated bombs in Laos. She took trips to Laos to meet families injured by bombies, sometimes bringing them to the United States to speak to the public. She also helped Lao refugee families in the United States to heal from the wreckage of war. "Oftentimes, people go through trauma, shame, and silence" after experiencing such tragic events, she explained. She wanted affected families to understand their pain and reject any thoughts that their suffering was justified. To achieve full restorative healing for all, Channapha gathered victims, US veterans who had participated in the bombings, and peace activists in panel discussion groups. Her goal was to boldly speak about the effects of warfare so that pain and suffering would not be passed on to future generations.

In addition to providing education and healing, Legacies' mission is to clear the unexploded bombs, also referred to as ordnance, from Laos. The year that the organization was formed, the US government earmarked $2 million per year for this task. Channapha lobbied politicians to increase this amount, and by 2016 it had expanded to

$30 million. Barack Obama, in the first trip to Laos by a US president, credited Legacies of War and Channapha as being instrumental in this outcome. Channapha has devoted her life to reconciling the past while also literally saving lives in Laos.

John Kneubuhl

(1920–1992)

Called the "spiritual father of Pacific Island theater," John Kneubuhl was an afakasi born in American Sāmoa, an island in the South Pacific. *Afakasi* refers to a person with Sāmoan and European ancestry. John's mother, a pianist, singer, and painter, was of Sāmoan ancestry, while his father, a navy surveyor, was a man from Iowa with Scottish and Welsh roots.

When John was three years old, he watched his two older brothers get into a boat and leave for Punahou School in Hawai'i. That experience left a deep mark on him, as he dealt with loneliness throughout his life. At age thirteen, he left for Punahou, where he excelled in track and field as well as piano. In the eighth grade, John met Dorothy "Dotsy" Schenk, a girl who directed him in the class play and would later become his life partner. The family friends he lived with in Hawai'i

I'm always the one who is going away and I'm always the one who is trying to get back home.

encouraged him to apply to Yale University, and he was accepted to the school's prestigious theater workshop.

John felt lonely at the university. His classmates would push him to say something in the Sāmoan language for their entertainment. These humiliating encounters did not prevent John from writing two plays that featured Indigenous Sāmoan stories. As he was able to pick up other languages easily, John, in addition to speaking English and Sāmoan, also learned how to speak Japanese and Tongan.

While he was in college, John attempted to get married to his childhood sweetheart, Dotsy. Yet in the state of Maryland, where her relatives lived, he could not marry her because there were antimiscegenation laws that denied marriage between people who were white and "Asiatic," a racial category that included Sāmoan people like John. Before John's graduation, the interracial couple got married in New Haven, Connecticut, where antimiscegenation laws were not in place.

After earning his bachelor's degree in creative writing, John served as a naval intelligence officer during World War II. He returned to Oʻahu and was recruited by the Honolulu Community Theatre to be an assistant director and playwright using traditional forms of Sāmoan theater like fale aitu in plays. In fale aitu, the lead actor becomes a spirit who often parodies authority figures.

While producing full-length Indigenous plays in Hawaiʻi, John had a growing family to support. To earn a living by writing, he had to travel to Hollywood, California, to write scripts. For twenty years he found great success as a writer for the most popular television shows, such as *Gunsmoke*, *The Fugitive*, *The Wild Wild West*, *Star Trek*, and *Hawaii Five-O*. John also directed and wrote a feature film, *Damien*, about a priest on the island of Molokaʻi who devoted his life to helping people afflicted with leprosy.

John later denigrated his episodic Hollywood work, even burning his teleplays. He said that he had "assumed a counterfeit voice, denying my own." He returned to Sāmoa in 1968 to pursue theater and restore his "real life." While teaching, he wrote a trilogy of plays that defined him as a Pacific Islander playwright. He established the American Sāmoa Community College and taught in Tonga and Hawai'i. Active in bilingual education, John strove to link the various Polynesian islands in his life and art to truly become "a citizen of the Polynesian world," instead of embracing only a single island.

The first play in his trilogy, *Think of a Garden*, which was John's last piece of writing, begins in 1929 American Sāmoa as a family deals with the colonial police killing of a Sāmoan chief and proindependence leader who was newly released from an Aotearoa/New Zealand prison. John passed away in Sāmoa a day before the first Sāmoan reading of the play was scheduled in the territorial capital of Pago Pago by his drama and writing group. Decades after his death, his plays continue to be produced throughout the Pacific. While John sometimes felt unseen in Hollywood, media scholars throughout the world study his television work for his portrayal of Sāmoan aesthetics and experiences in his characters and story lines.

Bruno Mars

(1985–)

Bruno Mars was born into a family of entertainers, with a father who is Puerto Rican Jewish and a mother who is Filipino Spanish. His given name was Peter Gene Hernandez, but his father gave him the nickname Bruno, after a champion pro wrestler. The family had a revue show at the Hilton Hotel, "Magic of Polynesia," which Bruno has described as "David Copperfield meets hula." As part of the show, Bruno's uncle impersonated Elvis, inspiring Bruno to become a mini Elvis, complete with the bouffant hair and sequined tight pantsuit with a turned-up collar. He even caught the attention of talent scouts and had a cameo in the movie *Honeymoon in Vegas*, in 1992, when he was seven years old.

Four years later, Bruno's parents divorced, splitting up the six children and ending the revue show. During one stretch, Bruno, his brother, and his father were virtually homeless, sleeping in a limousine and living in a one-room run-down building in a park. The resilient Bruno never felt the weight of these economic troubles because through the divorce, the family remained close. "We had each other," he said.

All Bruno knew was that he wanted to continue to perform music. At the age of eighteen, he moved to Los Angeles with his older brother, Eric "E-Panda" Hernandez, a noted drummer. Together they were part

of a cover band that played restaurants in San Fernando Valley. Within a year, Bruno was signed to a Motown contract. He thought that he was on his way to instant stardom but experienced a major disappointment when he was later dropped from the label. Bruno recalled comments from music executives: "He's got a Latin last name, but he doesn't speak Spanish. . . . 'What kind of music are you making?'"

He recalled his mixed background as being in the "gray zone." While some maintained that being in this gray zone meant artistic freedom, Bruno stated, "But it's not like that at all. It's actually the exact opposite." As a result, he had to forge his own path.

Having performed popular songs by beloved musicians since he was a child, Bruno understood what elements were necessary for a hit. He was introduced to another ambitious talent, Philip Lawrence, and they formed a songwriting partnership, the Smeezingtons. Later joined by producer Ari Levine, the team created hits for star artists such as Flo Rida, Lil Wayne, Wiz Khalifa, and CeeLo Green.

In 2009, nearly six years after moving to Hollywood, Bruno finally got his chance as a performer. His debut single, "Nothin' on You," also the debut single for rapper B.o.B, was released and soared to the top of the *Billboard* charts in the spring of 2010. From there, the floodgates opened. Bruno followed his debut with four other number-one hits—"Billionaire," "Just the Way You Are," "Grenade," and "Locked Out of Heaven"—a feat that no male artist had accomplished since Elvis Presley. He received his first invitation to perform at the Super Bowl Halftime Show in 2014.

Collaboration continues to be an essential signature of Bruno's success. He performs with his band, the Hooligans, featuring his songwriting partner, Lawrence, and his brother, Eric. Some of his most successful musical endeavors are the result of working closely with other artists. Not only did "Uptown Funk" win multiple Grammy Awards, but it was also number one on the charts for fourteen weeks, tying for the second-longest run at that time. It's been streamed more than two billion times.

It has to sound like who I am.
It has to sound like me.

A perfectionist, Bruno is known to completely scrap songs and start over if the music doesn't sound like him. In the studio, he spends thousands of hours selecting the perfect chords and instruments. He has also been described as a "nostalgia curator," seamlessly evoking the 1990s in hits like "24K," which has been embraced overseas, especially in the country of his mother's birth, the Philippines.

Bruno has established himself as a favorite among Hawaiʻi audiences, filling large Honolulu stadiums for concerts. After his 24K tour in Hawaiʻi, he donated twenty-four thousand Thanksgiving meals to families in need.

Carissa Moore

(1992–)

Born in Honolulu, Hawai'i, Carissa Kainani Moore was already being heralded as a world champion surfer at age fifteen. She was introduced to surfing by her father, a competitive swimmer, at age five and was spinning 360 degrees on waves when she was eight years old. At age eleven, she was the youngest surfer to compete in Hawai'i's Triple Crown.

By the time she was in high school, Carissa had beaten world champions and successfully competed against men, scoring a perfect 10 in an opening heat in an event in Mexico.

But Carissa had a secret: while starving herself in school, she'd binge eat at home and at night. The eating disorder came after she looked through lists celebrating the hottest surfer girls. While her peers were on that list, she wasn't, despite her accomplishments. As a teenager, she would think, "Why am I not hot? Why am I not beautiful? Why don't all these people think that I deserve to be on those lists?"

This insecurity didn't prevent Carissa from succeeding as a professional surfer. In 2010 she qualified for the World Surf League's Championship Tour, which is limited to only seventeen women competing in ten events. Being part of this elite group of surfers requires approximately 150 days of international travel in a single year.

The following season, Carissa, at age eighteen, became the youngest person—male or female—to win a surfing world title. She has since replicated this achievement multiple times. At age twenty-one, she was inducted into the Surfers' Hall of Fame, and Hawai'i declared January 4 to be Carissa Moore Day. She also secured a place on the 2021 USA Olympic surf team, being the only member of Native Hawaiian descent. She went on to win a gold medal, becoming the first woman to do so in the first-ever surfing event in the Olympics.

Being healthy and strong is the most beautiful thing.

Carissa's struggle with her body image changed when she entered her twenties. Feeling more confident and at peace with herself, she stated, "Don't try to compare yourself to anyone else. Don't try to be someone else. I think being healthy and strong is the most beautiful thing."

She started a female-empowerment nonprofit, Moore Aloha, which has three tenets: "Follow your dreams," "Be authentic," and "Help others." "I want to leave a message that I love surfing and get to do what I love, but I've also gone through a lot of challenges," said Carissa. "I want other girls to know I understand what they're going through."

Shirin Neshat

(1957–)

Even after getting a master's degree in fine arts from the University of California at Berkeley, where she studied painting and printmaking, Shirin Neshat felt her work was mediocre and lacked a clear vision. She decided to move to New York City, where she began working at the Storefront for Art and Architecture, a nonprofit laboratory for creative imagination. "That was the arts education that I needed," she said. It was not until she took the long journey back to her birthplace, Iran, after being separated from her people for more than fifteen years, that she discovered that art was the best and only way she could express how she felt.

Politics doesn't seem to escape people like me.

Shirin was born in Qazvin, a small city two hours from Tehran, the capital of Iran. Her father prioritized education for his daughters, and Shirin joined her older sister in the United States to complete her high school education in Los Angeles. While her sister returned to Iran, Shirin was an undergraduate at the University of California at Berkeley when the Islamic Revolution broke out in 1979, preventing Shirin from returning to Iran because it was too dangerous to travel. As a result, like other Iranians in the United States, Shirin became an exile, separated from her family and, at times, scapegoated for the hostage crisis at the US Embassy in Iran. "I found myself experiencing a huge loss in a country that I didn't really know very well. . . . I felt completely abandoned."

Then came the return to Iran in 1990. Shirin was shocked to see how a conservative Islamic government and a long war with Iraq had transformed her home country. Women covered themselves in veils as part of their religious practice. Trying to represent what she observed, Shirin worked with a photographer to create striking black-and-white images of veiled women—some of them of herself. Evoking the concept of women warriors, the subjects often posed with weapons, including guns. In calligraphy Shirin wrote Farsi poetry penned by Iranian women before and after the revolution over the exposed parts of the bodies, suggesting that there is more going on beneath the surface. The women in the photos could not be defined by only the veils they wore.

Often working with other collaborators from different countries, Shirin has moved from still photography to video to film to performance art. "I've never been afraid of taking risks and failing," she said. For her pioneering and experimental body of work, Shirin has received countless awards, including the Silver Lion Best Director Award in the Sixty-Sixth Venice International Film Festival in 2009.

All of her work is deeply personal, revealing her inner thoughts and anxieties. As she learned after her first return to Iran, "Wow, maybe I'm an artist at the end."

Amanda Nguyen

(1990–)

When Amanda Nguyen was sixteen years old, she had surgery to repair an abnormality in her heart. This first procedure failed, and she used a wheelchair for seven months in preparation for a second surgery. She was so weak at times that she couldn't feed herself. Yet the experience didn't defeat Amanda, the only child born to two Vietnamese refugees in Southern California.

Happily, the second surgery repaired the heart defect, and Amanda graduated as valedictorian from Centennial High School in Corona, California. After getting accepted to a number of elite universities, she decided to attend Harvard College in Cambridge, Massachusetts, with the intention of someday becoming an astronaut. At Harvard Amanda created the first student-written course on modern slavery. During her senior year in 2013, she survived a sexual assault.

Amanda was further traumatized when she learned about the policy regarding rape kits collected at hospitals for DNA evidence and used in the identification and prosecution of sex crimes. According to Massachusetts law, her rape kit would be kept on file for only six months, after which Amanda would have to petition the state every six months to keep it in storage, even though the statute of limitations for rape in the state is fifteen years.

"When I learned about this, I was left with a choice: either I could accept this injustice, or I could rewrite the law. I chose to rewrite the law," stated Amanda.

While working as a State Department liaison to the White House, she launched the nonprofit Rise (www.risenow.us), in November 2014, to achieve civil rights for sexual assault survivors. She created the Sexual Assault Survivors' Bill of Rights and successfully lobbied politicians to pass the bill in the US Senate. In October 2016, President Obama signed it into law, thus ensuring that rape kits in federal cases will be automatically preserved without charge for the duration of the statute of limitations. Amanda, who was nominated for the 2019 Nobel Peace Prize, is also at work to get the Survivors' Bill of Rights passed in every state.

No one is powerless when we come together.
No one can make us invisible when
we demand to be seen.

In 2020 during the height of COVID-19, anti-Asian hate crimes rose 150 percent. Activists like Amanda connected this increase to the unjust scapegoating of Asian Americans, a phenomenon that has continued during bleak moments throughout US history. Amanda turned to social media to address the lack of mainstream media's coverage of the violence aimed at Asian Americans. On Instagram Live, she delivered an impassioned message: "Our community is being attacked. And we are dying to be heard." The post received three million views in twenty-four hours.

Through Rise, she started Survivor Safe Haven, a program involving essential services like grocery stores to step in and assist Asian

Americans experiencing racist violence. Key in Amanda's strategy is to increase the visibility of Asian American stories in both media and political circles.

Seeking to help young people to "pen their own civil rights bills," Amanda's organization launched Rise Justice Labs. A civil rights incubator, Rise Justice Labs provides at a minimum $5,000 and a twelve-week training program for organizers to take concrete steps to make changes in specific issues that concern them. At its center is Hopeanomics™ with the catchphrase "Hope is contagious." Amanda acts to make her optimism a reality.

Naomi Osaka

(1997–)

---

*I want to use my platform
to advocate for change.*

Born in Osaka, Japan, to a Japanese mother and Haitian father, Naomi Osaka and her older sister, Mari, were given their mother's maiden name as a last name. Watching Serena Williams and her older sister Venus play tennis on television inspired Naomi's father to introduce her and her sister to the sport. When Naomi was three, the family moved to Long Island, New York, to be close to her paternal grandparents and lived there until 2006 when they moved to Florida so she could train for tennis.

At the age of fourteen, she became a pro player under the Women's Tennis Association. She was ranked 430th in the world. In three years, with her trademark propulsive serves, aggressive baseline play, and steadiness, her ranking went up to 40th, and she was named Newcomer of the Year.

In 2018 Naomi faced her childhood idol, Serena Williams, for the US Open Championship. Prevailing in high-pressure matches, she became the first Japanese player to win a Grand Slam tournament. Naomi was twenty years old at the time. Regarding facing her hero, she said, "I just blocked out all my emotions and thought about playing against the ball, like every ball that came across the net was my opponent."

In 2019 Naomi won her second Grand Slam tournament—this time the Australian Open. She became the number-one women's tennis player in the world. During that period, she also became the highest-paid female athlete.

One of her Japanese sponsors produced an anime TV commercial with Naomi depicted with pale skin even though she is a person of color. Highly criticized, the ad was pulled by the company. Naomi, who is a Japanese citizen living in the United States, explained that she considers herself a Japanese Haitian American. "I always grew up with a little bit more Japanese heritage and culture, but I'm Black," she said.

With her biracial and international background, Naomi has defied labels that have been placed on her. She is a fan of gaming, fashion, and photography. Although soft-spoken, she has found creative ways—whether on social media or other platforms—to express her opinions of what matters to her.

She returned to play the US Open in 2020, during the middle of the COVID-19 pandemic. As players were required to wear masks when they entered the court, Naomi wore a different mask to her seven matches, each with the names of Black victims of racist violence. Without having to say a word, Naomi found a way to generate conversation as the media televised her appearance.

She went on to win that Grand Slam event. As in-person spectators were barred from attending the tournament, Naomi lay on the surface of the court with her eyes focused on the sky. Referencing other champions who took that position, she said, "I've always wanted to see what they saw."

Naomi has also created conversations regarding the mental health of athletes. In a move that initiated much international debate, she chose to skip the press conferences at the French Open to exercise self-care. Subjected to financial sanctions and media criticism, she eventually dropped out of the tournament. She has since advocated for changes in the traditional press-conference format, which can be emotionally taxing on athletes. "It's okay not to be okay," she said as an encouragement to prioritize one's mental health.

Craig Santos Perez

(1980 –)

Craig Santos Perez is a native CHamoru born and raised on the island of Guam, known by its people as Guåhan. Guåhan, the southernmost island of the Marianas chain, has been controlled by outside powers since the sixteenth century: Spain, the United States, and Japan. CHamoru are the Indigenous people of the Marianas Archipelago.

Craig grew up in a small village where electricity outages were common. When the lights went out, the extended family gathered around his father's barbecue, where Craig learned of relatives who were sick from the toxic poisons disseminated into the environment by the US military. He also became aware of how colonization impacted his culture. For example, his grandparents were punished in Guåhan schools for speaking the CHamoru language. Outside of his home, Craig himself was taught entirely in English and used English exclusively in public.

*Poetry is like a prayer
that believes in resurrection.*

When Craig was fifteen, in 1995, his family migrated to California. This move was common among CHamoru seeking opportunities beyond the military, and today more Native people live outside of the island than on it.

On the first day of his new high school, a teacher asked Craig where he was from. After Craig answered Guam, the teacher said, "I've never heard of Guam [Guåhan]. Prove it exists."

Craig pointed to an empty space on a world map. "I'm from this invisible island," he replied.

The teacher continued asking Craig insensitive questions about whether he was a US citizen. "You speak English well," the teacher concluded, "with almost no accent."

Reflecting on this childhood incident, Craig later wrote, "And isn't this what it means to be from an unincorporated territory: to be foreign in a domestic sense. To be invisible."

To alleviate his homesickness and to feel connected to Guåhan, Craig began writing poetry. In contrast to his earlier experience, another high school teacher, poet Thomas Seaton, inspired him to continue to study literature. He did so, gaining his bachelor's degree at the University of Redlands, and then entering the master of fine arts program at the University of San Francisco, where he was mentored by the editor of Omnidawn Publishing, which later published some of his poetry collections.

Craig pursued a doctorate in comparative ethnic studies from the University of California at Berkeley. He is currently a professor in the English Department at the University of Hawai'i at Mānoa, where he teaches creative writing, eco-poetry, and Pacific literature.

In Craig's own creative work, the CHamoru language is starting to reappear in small ways as words from the natural world or prayers. Regarding the role of the writer, he said, "Stories are canoes/ves-

sels that carry our languages, customs, values, practices, knowledge, memories, dreams, hopes, hurts, traumas, histories, beliefs, and much more."

Craig's various literary awards and recognitions have led to fellowships to teach in Guåhan. After he read his poetry to an honors English class on Guåhan, he discovered that one of the students was crying.

"What's wrong?" he asked.

This was the first time for the student to see her culture reflected in a book. "I just thought we weren't worthy of literature."

While tackling topics like US militarism in his writing, Craig has found, "Poetry is the place where I can speak my truth. Even if you can't talk about these difficult things in person, here's a space where we can feel free to discuss it."

Mau Piailug

(1932–2010)

The ancient navigators of the Pacific did not depend on a compass, chart, or sextant—a tool for measuring altitudes in navigation—to determine how to travel from one island to another. Instead, these men, called palu, relied on the observation of the sea, sky, and stars to determine their course through waters. Pius Piailug, more commonly known as Mau, which means "Strength" in his native Satawal, was part of this important seafaring family lineage. He could have been one of the last palu navigators, but chose to train a new generation outside of his bloodline and culture.

Mau began his training as a wayfinder at the age of one in Satawal, a small Micronesian island, only a mile and a half long and a mile wide, with only five hundred residents. His grandfather, a master navigator, took Mau, his chosen one, to tide pools at different parts of the island. They sat and observed the movement of the water, wind, and ocean. At age four, Mau and his grandfather went sailing in a canoe. Mau would get seasick, but his grandfather put him in the water to cure him of motion sickness. It worked.

When Mau was about twenty, he was formally initiated in a sacred and private Pwo ritual to be palu, a master navigator. Another Pwo ceremony would not be held for thirty-nine years.

In the 1970s, when Mau was in his forties, the Polynesian Voyaging Society, a nonprofit group in Honolulu, Hawaiʻi, was formed to replicate the way of early Polynesian travel without Western instruments from Tahiti to Hawaiʻi, just as it had been done four thousand years ago. A customary double-hulled canoe, the *Hōkūleʻa*, was built. All they needed was an expert navigator to guide the vessel twenty-three hundred nautical miles from Hawaiʻi to Tahiti. There were a handful of palu in Micronesia, but only Mau was willing to share his ancient knowledge with the crew. This would be a hazardous journey, but Mau was willing to take the risk as the *Hōkūleʻa*'s captain. "If I have courage it is because I have faith in the knowledge of my ancestors," he said.

In 1976 the *Hōkūleʻa* set sail. For a month, Mau sat in the same spot of the canoe, the image of Tahiti in his head. They finally reached their destination and were welcomed by seventeen thousand Tahitians—half of the population of the entire island—overwhelmed by the crew's amazing accomplishment. Mau, however, was not happy. The crew had been divided on the motivations for the trip. One side saw it as a scientific experiment, while the other went for cultural reasons. The divided motivations heightened tensions on the sea, even resulting in a fistfight. Mau refused to journey back with them, vowing never to travel with the Polynesian Voyaging Society again.

The *Hōkūleʻa* was launched without Mau in 1978, but with tragic results. The canoe capsized, and one of the crew members, the legendary surfer Eddie Aikau, was lost at sea and never found. (*Note:* See Eddie Aikau biography.)

A third voyage was planned for 1980 with its navigator, Nainoa Thompson, a Native Hawaiian with a bachelor's degree in ocean science from the University of Hawaiʻi at Mānoa. In spite of his education, Nainoa was insecure in his abilities. He was able to convince Mau to help him. "I will train you to find Tahiti because I don't want you to die," Mau told him. Nainoa became the first Native Hawaiian person to successfully navigate a double-hulled canoe to a Polynesian island without the use of Western instruments since they were introduced. Mau traveled with him as an observer.

*I have laid the stick
that connects people together.*

Motivated to keep the art of palu alive, Mau shared his knowledge with other Polynesian people outside of Micronesia. "I have laid the stick that connects people together," he said. He wanted Pacific Islanders to remain in unity.

Fifty-six years after his initiation, Mau inducted sixteen people, including Nainoa and four other Native Hawaiian navigators, into the Pwo in 2007. That year Clay Bertelmann of Nā Kālai Waʻa gave Mau a double-hulled canoe, the *Alingano Maisu*, which means "Ripe Breadfruit Blown from a Tree in a Storm," referring to his openness and the sharing of something good.

Keanu Reeves

(1964–)

Actor Keanu Reeves, whose first name means "Cool Breeze" in 'Ōlelo Hawai'i (the Hawaiian language), has been described as the "nicest man in Hollywood." Despite depicting assassins like John Wick in blockbuster movies, the superstar has been identified as a respectful and caring person in viral social media posts. His humility is exceptional, especially in light of the box-office success of his movies, which has exceeded $3 billion.

Keanu was born in Beirut, Lebanon, to a British mother who worked as a costume designer and a Chinese Hawaiian father. From ages six to twenty, he lived in Toronto with his mother and sister. Bitten by the acting bug, he dropped out of high school and performed onstage and in a few made-for-TV movies before landing a minor role on *Youngblood*, a hockey movie shot in Canada. Afterward, Keanu headed for Los Angeles to establish a career in film. He snagged roles in critically acclaimed movies such as *River's Edge* and the Oscar-nominated *Dangerous Liaisons*. But it was the time-travel comedy *Bill & Ted's Excellent Adventure*, in which he played half of a duo of underachieving California teenagers, that launched him to star status in 1989.

Since then Keanu has developed a cult following for iconic characters in movies like the FBI/surf-heist movie *Point Break*, directed by

Kathryn Bigelow, and the *Matrix* and *John Wick* franchises, among others. He is known for his dedication to training for action movies and has helped launch the careers of stuntmen turned directors and producers. His down-to-earth persona was also celebrated on social media, as a 2010 stock photo of Keanu sitting alone on a park bench eating a sandwich started viral #sadKeanu memes.

I'm not looking for a red carpet to walk, and I'm not trying to have a celebrity footprint.

While the public may label Keanu's ethnicity in different ways, he self-identifies as a person of color. The groundbreaking Netflix Asian American rom-com *Always Be My Maybe*, starring Ali Wong and Randall Park, featured Keanu as the ultimate cool love interest.

He stated, "I hope that whatever opportunities I've had, or the work that I'm doing, in some way can entertain and can also—I don't want to say teach—but have something of value come out of it."

Keanu has explored other creative endeavors, such as playing bass in an alternative rock band, Dogstar, in the 1990s. He also started a small press, X Artists' Books, in Los Angeles with his partner, artist Alexandra Grant. His interest in the published word and images has extended to comic books. In 2021 Boom! Studios released the actor's twelve-issue limited series about a half-man, half-immortal warrior who has walked the earth for eighty thousand years. The *BRZRKR* comic book even pays tribute to the #sadKeanu meme in one panel, evidence of Keanu's good sense of humor.

Lakshmi Singh

(ca. 1972–)

When public radio newscaster Lakshmi Singh was very young, she struggled not only with shyness but also with stuttering. Like most children and even adults, she feared embarrassing herself in front of her peers, specifically her classmates. Over time, she learned strategies to help control her speech. In high school in New York, she pursued classes in forensics, debate, and drama.

She was reciting a poem onstage one day when her teacher said, "I can't hear you."

Lakshmi tried speaking louder, but she still couldn't be heard. "Shout, just yell," the teacher instructed her.

She did. "It was exhilarating. That's when I started to gain confidence," she said. She had found her voice.

After high school, Lakshmi attended Syracuse University's S. I. Newhouse School of Public Communications and the College of Arts and Sciences, where she studied Latin American studies, Spanish, and broadcast journalism. She was introduced to a local commercial radio station but discovered that on-air spots for women were hard to get. Instead, she honed her radio skills at a public radio station, WAER, in Syracuse, which Lakshmi described as one of the best training grounds in the country for young journalists. At WAER she learned to write, interview, and use recording tools like microphones. "You take a story and allow it to breathe," she said.

She went on to work for various local public radio stations before becoming a midday newscaster and a guest host for National Public Radio, which she joined in 2000. In addition to working with various media outlets, she was a regular contributor to the magazine shows *Latino USA* and *Soundprint Media*, working as a field reporter and documentary producer, leading her to Central America and the West Indies.

You can't dictate who I am.
You can't dictate how I pronounce my name.
You cannot dictate what my background is.
I call the shots on that one.

Lakshmi has Indo-Trinidadian roots from her father and Puerto Rican roots from her mother. Her multiracial identity often led to her feeling alienated. However, she discovered that her mixed ethnic identity actually served her well in journalism, providing "a certain level of sensitivity" to interview subjects who also felt that they didn't belong.

"Alienation also came from me," Lakshmi admitted. For instance, she has been criticized for the pronunciation of her first name, which represents a goddess in the Hindu religion. Lakshmi says her name "LAK-shmee," not "LUK-shmee," as it is more traditionally pronounced. She prefers to follow the way her paternal Indo-Trinidadian grandmother said her name.

Being one of the most recognizable voices on public radio, Lakshmi has inspired would-be journalists who have also felt like outsiders.

Vishavjit Singh

(1971–)

Cartoonist and software engineer Vishavjit Singh planned to be Captain America for only one day for a photo shoot on the streets of New York City, but he quickly discovered that the red, white, and blue uniform was the most visible way for him to challenge stereotypes regarding the Sikh people.

Originating in the region of present-day India and Pakistan, Sikhism is the fifth-largest major religion in the world. Since only five hundred thousand followers live in the United States, misconceptions abound. Traditional Sikhs don five articles of faith, including unshorn hair. Many also wear turbans as a message of equality and a statement of self-respect.

Confuse them so they can't box me in.

Vishavjit was born in Washington, DC, but grew up in Delhi, India. As a young teenager and avid doodler, he witnessed the 1984 Indian military attacks on Sikh houses of worship. After high school, he followed his family's instruction and pursued studies in the sciences in the

United States. He received degrees in biology and anthropology at the University of California at Santa Barbara and graduate degrees in epidemiology and biostatistics. Early during this time of academic activity, he did not prioritize his faith as a Sikh, but developed a passion for books. "Words became my time machine, my savior and guide," he wrote.

Recommitting himself to following the Sikh path after studying Eastern philosophy in college, he stopped cutting his hair and began wearing a turban. He was working as a computer programmer in Connecticut at the time of the 9/11 attacks in New York City. Islamophobia spilled out to other little-known religions in the United States like Sikhism, and Vishavjit found himself the target of religious and racial hatred.

To combat this intolerance, he returned to his love of drawing and created cartoons with Sikh characters and stories, housed at Sikhtoons .com. "I'm creating characters who look like me because I don't see characters who look like me anywhere in America," he said.

After the 2012 massacre on a Sikh house of worship by a white supremacist in Wisconsin, a photographer approached Vishavjit about bringing his cartoon of a Sikh American superhero to life. Wearing his turban, he became Captain America in Manhattan. While the majority embraced him, posing with him for selfies, some observers called him derogatory names. He was even able to sit for photographs in a New York City fire engine.

Vishavjit continues to educate people "with compassion" through art, storytelling, and public speaking engagements. Through daily meditation, Vishavjit unlearns the biased narratives reflected in the outside world.

Thenmozhi Soundararajan

(1976 –)

Thenmozhi Soundararajan was in the fifth grade in Los Angeles when she learned about a family secret from her mother—that they were Dalit, previously known as "Untouchable," under the caste system. At the top were Brahmins, mainly teachers and intellectuals, historically known as the priestly class, followed by warriors and rulers, traders, and menial workers. Dalits were even below that, outside of the main system.

People's caste, determined by birth, often dictated how they were treated by people in society, whom they married, and what jobs were available to them. Sometimes their life could be threatened because of their social status. Thenmozhi's family members were vulnerable to both caste discrimination and bias—and even violence just for being part of the Dalit class.

While caste is strong in Thenmozhi's homelands in South Asia, it is here, too, in America. Both of her parents were the first Dalit doctors in their community and tried their best to start a new life here. But because they saw caste discrimination here, they decided to hide their caste to survive. Watching her family struggle with the fear of being discovered made Thenmozhi determined to study caste and work to end it for all South Asian Americans. That is why Thenmozhi applied to

University of California Berkeley. But she could not keep silent. For her college thesis, she made a film on caste and violence against women, "outing" herself as a Dalit for the first time.

She was not alone. A classmate, emotionally moved by the film, confided that she was also a Dalit. "It was vital I kept growing as a storyteller because it was only in our stories that we could be free—exactly what I had hoped for with my film," Thenmozhi said.

This revelation, however, would come at a cost. Many Indians on campus were part of the upper or dominant castes and rejected Thenmozhi for being Dalit, even on US soil. The response back in India was even more severe. Friends stopped talking to Thenmozhi's family. "I even received hate mail and death threats. My coming of age and recognition of my family's identity was viewed as something sinister," she wrote.

Sometimes you have to decide to be strong first, and then strength comes along.

After graduation, Thenmozhi was inspired to create a media training and resource center, Third World Majority, where she led sessions in countries such as France, Tunisia, Venezuela, Brazil, South Africa, and India. Merging storytelling with advocacy, she has written poetry, produced a blues album, and curated photo exhibitions to educate about Dalit peoples. Her work with the Massachusetts Institute of Technology Center for Reflective Community Practice led Thenmozhi to study narrative filmmaking at the University of Southern California School of Cinematic Arts and receive her master's degree in fine arts.

Calling herself the Dalit Diva, she began to reach out and organize

Dalits, whose numbers are estimated at two hundred and sixty million throughout the world. She became the founder and director of Equality Labs and built networks between South Asian and caste-oppressed immigrants and Black, Indigenous, and Asian movements. In 2016 Equality Labs conducted the first survey on caste discrimination in the United States and discovered that one in four Dalits surveyed reported facing physical and verbal assault. One in three experienced educational discrimination, and two in three faced job discrimination.

Thenmozhi has been shining a light specifically on employment practices in California's Silicon Valley, whose high-tech multinational companies hire many workers from India. Her concern is that Dalits may experience bullying and discrimination by supervisors and coworkers who belong to higher castes. She advocates that caste be treated as a protected category in civil rights laws. She writes, "The time to end caste discrimination—both in the United States and around the world—is now."

Teresia Teaiwa

(1968–2017)

Poet and Pacific scholar Teresia Teaiwa's first teachers were her parents. Her African American mother, originally from Washington, DC, was a high school teacher, and her father, born in Kiribati (pronounced "Kiri-bas"), an independent island country located in the Pacific, was a government worker. Teresia was born in Honolulu, Hawai'i, but raised in Fiji, where the family moved to in 1969.

In secondary school, Teresia ran the 1,500-meter race and came in last. "My mum was in the grandstand watching. She was so proud because I finished the race," Teresia said. That taught Teresia that whenever she starts an endeavor, she needs to always finish.

Because her father worked for the Fiji Ministry of Agriculture, Teresia and her family moved from island to island. Her love for the various Pacific Islands continued to grow. She was captivated by each region's diversity, beauty, and pain.

The pain came from colonization and militarization. For example, Kiribati, her father's birthplace, was a British colony. After World War II, the British forced three generations of her father's family, along with other islanders, to move to another British colony, Fiji, because the government wanted to exploit the mining of phosphate in Kiribati.

Teresia traveled to the other side of the world to study, eventually earning her doctorate and becoming an antinuclear activist.

"The Pacific Ocean is the largest single geographical space on the planet," she said. "Our ancestors found it, settled it, and it's a gift that we have a responsibility to look after with our minds, hearts, and our spirits."

She also began working on oral histories about the growing presence of Fijian women soldiers.

Teresia observed that in modern Fiji, women enter the military for economic reasons rather than for societal liberation. While she advocated demilitarization of the Pacific Islands, Teresia felt a closer look at the woman soldier in Fiji could inform the next best steps toward this goal.

*We sweat and cry salt water,
so we know that the ocean is
really in our blood.*

In 1996 Teresia turned down a job with the environmental group Greenpeace to pursue what would become her lifelong passion: teaching. Her first lecturer position was with the University of the South Pacific in Fiji. She then moved to Aotearoa/New Zealand to teach classes for the world's first undergraduate major in Pacific studies at Victoria University.

Teresia found this task an "audacious undertaking." How could she, a single person, address the diversity of the Pacific Islands region, in which twelve hundred Indigenous languages are spoken? She adopted a concept used in Micronesian navigation in which the canoe is stationary, while islands move toward it. In other words, her students could begin with their own location and heritage and find connections to the rest of the Pacific.

Her creative sensibilities bled into her teaching. While in the academic world, Teresia was also publishing poetry and plays, representing Kiribati at a Poetry Parnassus festival in London in 2012. Her solo recorded collection of poetry, *I Can See Fiji*, was described by a reviewer as "groundbreaking." At Victoria University, she introduced an initiative in which students could integrate art and performance into their class assignments. She was a personable and hands-on educator, known for connecting students and telling them to "stop selling [themselves] short."

Her untimely death in 2017 from pancreatic cancer at age forty-eight shocked and saddened the Pacific Islander and academic communities upon which she had a profound impact. On National Poetry Day in 2018, Teresia's poem "Mother" was released in translation in thirty languages, becoming "Multilingual Mother" in this new incarnation.

Philip Vera Cruz

(1904–1994)

Philip Vera Cruz and other Filipino men in central California played a pivotal role in the fight for farmworkers' rights. Their labor strike in the grape fields in Delano in 1965 led to the creation of the United Farm Workers union under the leadership of Cesar Chavez and Dolores Huerta. Philip served as the UFW vice president, the highest-ranking Filipino in the union.

Philip was born in the Philippines on Christmas Day 1904. At this time, the Philippines, comprising thousands of islands near China, was a US colony, which meant that Filipinos were US nationals. Thousands of Filipino bachelors moved to Hawai'i and the continental United States from the early 1900s to the 1930s to fill low-wage jobs. These people were called manongs, a term for a beloved older brother or relative. Since there were antimiscegenation laws in California, which barred ethnic minorities who lived there from marrying white people, many manongs, with some exceptions, remained single for the rest of their lives.

When Philip arrived in the United States in 1926, he intended to return to the Philippines someday after earning money to help his family. In the United States he worked as a migrant farmworker in North Dakota and a restaurant busboy in Spokane, Washington, and Chicago. He was unable to finish college for financial reasons. Philip eventually settled in Delano, California, known for its rows of grapevines.

Life was hard. He and other Filipino farmworkers sometimes worked out in the fields picking produce ten hours a day for seventy to eighty cents an hour. The labor camps were rife with mosquitoes and cockroaches, and one time the workers ended up digging a hole for a toilet.

While Philip was in the United States, his father died in the Philippines. Philip continued to send money to the rest of the family. "I couldn't tell them some of the truths about my life here because I wanted to make them believe that America was [as] good as I believed before I left. I had to struggle to make it good, at least for myself," he said.

The most important thing is getting people together.

Philip was drafted during World War II when he was in his late thirties. Instead of being sent into combat, he was released with other Filipinos to work on farms to provide food for the nation.

In 1948 Philip experienced his first major strike on an asparagus farm in a small town in Northern California. It was led by Filipino Americans. The larger movement to organize farmworkers, however, was slow. Unions and organizations were often divided by ethnicity. Philip said, "In my own way of reasoning about labor unions, I think the most important thing is getting people together."

By deciding to strike in Delano on September 8, 1965, Filipino American farmworkers sparked a larger labor movement, causing competing factions to come together to form the UFW, which would become the most well-known and powerful farmworker union in the United States.

Philip stayed with the union for twelve years. He was able to participate in the establishment of a retirement home for manong farmworkers in Delano. It was named Agbayani Village, after farmworker Paulo Agbayani, who died while on a union picket line in 1967.

He took his first visit back to the Philippines in 1987 when he was presented an award for his lifelong service by President Corazon Aquino.

Hinaleimoana Kwai Kong Wong-Kalu

(1972–)

Hinaleimoana Kwai Kong Wong-Kalu, also known as Hina Wong-Kalu, has been inspired by matriarchs of Hawai'i since childhood. "I remember my maternal grandmother putting her hand over mine," Hina stated. "My name at that time was Collin, and she said: 'Collin, you have to study hard now. One day you are going to become a teacher.'"

These words were prescient, as Hina, also inspired by hula instructors, or kumu, became a teacher of Hawaiian arts and culture. Hina was born in the Nu'uanu district of O'ahu to a Chinese American father and a Hawaiian mother who was also of Portuguese and British descent. The youngest of four children, Hina found that Hawaiian studies—the language, culture, and music—at Kamehameha School was a refuge to explore the concept of māhū, or hina, a third way to consider gender. Rather than a female and male binary, māhū embraces both feminine and masculine characteristics.

In 1993 Collin officially transitioned to become Hinaleimoana. She studied at the University of Hawai'i at Mānoa and for thirteen years

taught at Hālau Lōkahi, a public charter school that celebrated Native Hawaiian culture, history, and education. At Hālau Lōkahi, Hinaleimoana mentored students to learn traditional chants and dance as well as to impart "a genuine understanding of unconditional acceptance and respect." For her work in training two generations of Hawaiian children, she received the Ellison S. Onizuka Memorial Award from the National Education Association.

Respect for past generations continued to be an integral theme in Hina's life. She became involved with the Oʻahu Island Burial Council, which oversees the management of Native Hawaiian burial sites and ancestral remains, and eventually served as the group's chair. In this role, Hina was able to get opposing sides—developers and descendants—to reach consensus when remains were discovered on construction sites. Observers pointed out that her negotiating power lies in her ability to completely be herself.

Protesters seeking to protect the Maunakea on the Big Island from the encroachment of a giant telescope have turned to one of Hina's original songs for inspiration. Called "Kū Haʻaheo E Kuʻu Hawaiʻi—Stand Tall My Hawaiʻi," Hina's composition, which was also performed by a choir at Kamehameha, featured the lyrics "The new dawn for our people of Hawaiʻi is upon us."

Hina has also been at the center of two groundbreaking movies. One was a documentary, *Kumu Hina*, that spotlighted Hina's work at the Hālau Lōkahi, her māhū identity, and her personal struggles. *Kumu Hina* won numerous awards and had an Independent Lens PBS television premiere in 2015. In 2020 Hinaleimoana collaborated with the *Kumu Hina* filmmakers to codirect and coproduce an animated short film, *Kapaemahu,* which tells the story of four māhū healers who traveled from another Polynesian island to Waikīkī Beach thousands of years ago. Four large stones representing the legendary healers are preserved today inside a City and County of Honolulu monument on the beach. Narrated in ʻŌlelo Hawaiʻi (the Hawaiian language), *Kapaemahu* made the Oscar short list for best animated feature.

That's what I hope most to leave with my students: A genuine understanding of unconditional acceptance and respect. To me that's the true meaning of aloha.

Hina now teaches Hawaiian language, culture, and history to people who are incarcerated in two correctional facilities on Oʻahu. "The goal of my class is to help them understand how culture will not only ground them in what they do now and what they do moving forward, but how it will help sustain them, once they get out," she said.

Chien-Shiung Wu

(1912–1997)

Called the "first lady of physics," Chien-Shiung Wu was born in Jiangsu, a coastal province just north of Shanghai, China. Her mother was a teacher, and her father, an engineer by training, also founded and led one of the first elementary schools in China to admit girls. Her father encouraged Chien-Shiung to seek knowledge.

After studying at her father's school, she graduated to a boarding school and enrolled in a program that emphasized the humanities for a career in teaching. Chien-Shiung's passion, however, was science, and she started to study mathematics, physics, and chemistry on her own. In 1930 she eventually ended up at the National Central University in Nanjing with an intention of majoring in mathematics. By this time, Marie Curie's discoveries in radioactive isotopes had revolutionized the field of physics. Inspired by Curie and intrigued by the possibilities in science, Chien-Shiung changed her focus to physics. She graduated at the top of her class with a bachelor of science degree in 1934.

After graduating, Chien-Shiung taught while also conducting her first experiment at a physics laboratory. She worked under a female professor who had recently returned from studying in the United States. That professor encouraged Chien-Shiung to go to the United States and learn from top scientists there. With financial help from an uncle, she entered the University of California at Berkeley as a doctoral student and studied the fission products of uranium. She was especially skilled in developing appropriate instruments to make accurate measurements.

After receiving her PhD in 1940, Chien-Shiung wanted to remain as a professor at Berkeley but learned that tenure-track positions were often closed to women of color. She obtained a teaching position at an all-women's school, Smith College, and then became the first female instructor in the physics department at Yale University. In 1944 she was invited to join the government's Manhattan Project at Columbia

Why should we not encourage more girls to [study] science?

University. The Manhattan Project was created for the development of nuclear weapons during World War II. Chien-Shiung joined Columbia University's lab to develop the process for separating uranium metal into isotopes by gaseous diffusion. Also working to improve Geiger counters for measuring radiation levels, she might have been the only Chinese person to have worked on the Manhattan Project.

Chien-Shiung, who was offered a teaching position at Columbia, began investigating beta decay, which occurs when the nucleus of one element changes into another element. In 1956 two male physicists approached her to design a special experiment to validate their theory about the conservation of parity, specifically that identical nuclear particles do not act alike during beta decay. Chien-Shiung meticulously conducted a set of experiments in Washington, DC, proving that these two scientists' theory was correct. In 1957 they won the Nobel Prize, but Chien-Shiung was excluded from this honor. She felt that her contributions were not recognized because she was a woman. Later, she would say at a Massachusetts Institute of Technology symposium: "I wonder whether the tiny atoms and nuclei, or the mathematical symbols, or the DNA molecules have any preference for either masculine or feminine treatment."

Chien-Shiung continued to work as a professor at Columbia and eventually became the first woman to hold a tenured faculty position in the university's physics department. Her research was recognized with the highest awards in science. In 1975 she was the first woman to serve as president of the American Physical Society. After retirement she worked to encourage young women to enter the scientific fields. She suffered a stroke and died at her home in New York City in 1997. A bronze statue marks where her ashes are buried in the courtyard of the girls school that she attended in China.

Jerry Yang

(1968–)

Jerry Yang was filing books at a library while attending Stanford University when he began to understand how information was sorted and categorized. That was the early foundation of Yahoo! Inc., one of the first online navigational guides to the World Wide Web in 1994.

Jerry was given the name Chih-Yuan Yang at birth in Taipei, Taiwan, by his parents, who had fled mainland China. When he was two, his father passed away. His mother, Lily, had to raise Jerry and his younger brother, Ken, on her own as an English professor at a university in Taipei. As Taiwan was under martial law at this time, Lily eventually moved her two boys to the United States for a better future. They settled in East San Jose, California, when Jerry was ten years old.

No place for hate in our society.

Practically the only English word Jerry and his brother knew at the time was *shoe*. "We got made fun of a lot at first," he said. But Jerry caught on quickly and excelled in school, being not only named class valedictorian but also elected student-body president.

Jerry graduated from nearby Stanford University in California with bachelor's and master's degrees in electrical engineering in four years.

He then entered the university's PhD program, specializing in computer-aided design, better known as CAD, software. On an exchange program in Japan, Jerry bonded with another doctoral student, David Filo. This friendship would transform the way we use personal computers today.

First developing a program with Mosaic, the new software at the time, they updated statistics on their favorite National Basketball Association basketball players. This passion became more serious as they created Jerry's and David's Guide to the World Wide Web, which was renamed Yahoo, an acronym for "Yet Another Hierarchical Officious Oracle."

By the fall of 1994, the search engine received its millionth hit. A year later Yahoo! was incorporated. Rejecting traditional corporate titles, Jerry and David each became the "Chief Yahoo," and another Stanford student, Tim Brady, became their first employee. In 1996 the company went public on the New York Stock Exchange, and on the first day of trading Yahoo! was valued at $848 million.

Yahoo! continued to expand its internet business, and in 2000 revenue reached $1 billion. Since that time, Google has replaced companies like AOL and Yahoo! to become the predominant web service, and Jerry eventually left his leadership positions at Yahoo! But before his exit, he successfully negotiated two of the biggest investments in the internet: Yahoo! Japan and Alibaba Group.

He and his wife, Akiko Yamazaki, now devote themselves to public service. Jerry is one of the founding board members of the Asian American Foundation, which seeks to address the lack of investment in the Asian American community. He is behind "Decoding Hate," a web-based digital project that tracked the incidents of anti-Asian hate during the pandemic through social media posts. "You can't fight what you can't measure, which is why efforts to track hate are so critical," he said. Regarding the foundation, he hopes that it will address long-term problems and look after all Asian Americans in the United States.

Reflection Guide

by Andrea Kim Neighbors and
Healoha Johnston

Smithsonian Asian Pacific American Center

We *Are Here* features the stories of Asian American and Pacific Islander people whose experiences suggest that everyday acts of compassion, creativity, commitment, and activism can change the course of one's life, can transform the relationship one has to the environment, and can impact the lives of others by expanding the social, cultural, and political landscapes. Their stories are indicative of struggles—personal and collective—and ongoing resistance that insist upon the humanity of all people. This book is an expression of solidarity with the distinct communities and identities represented throughout the text under the umbrella term *Asian American and Pacific Islander,* or *AAPI.*

REFLECTION QUESTIONS

Reflecting on the stories you have read throughout this book, consider the following questions below as a guide for organizing a conversation with your peers, friends, family, and community. These questions can also be used for your own quiet reflection.

REFLECTION GUIDE

- Which stories in this book did you connect with the most, and why?

- What surprised you about these stories? What new information did you learn in this book that you did not know before?

- If you could invite some of the people in this book to have a meal with you . . .

   - Whom would you invite?

   - What would you ask them? What would you talk about?

   - What would you want them to learn about you?

   - What kind of meal would you have with them? What does this meal express about you and your story?

- At this meal, what would you tell your guests about what you have learned about Asian American and Pacific Islander histories that you did not know before?

- What are some everyday acts of compassion, creativity, commitment, and activism that you take part in?

   - Are there people in this book who share similar everyday acts with you?

REFLECTION ACTIVITY IDEAS

Using a journal, a variety of art-making materials, or shared notes with a group, write or visualize your answers to each question above. You can use any method that helps you process information and new ideas. After you spend some time looking back at what you have written or created, share it with people who are important to you. What did you learn about yourself through this process, and what did you learn about others?

Our intention is for these stories to express the global interconnections of AAPI histories and stories through family, friendship, mentorship, and the environment. We also hope that this book and reflection guide spark a journey to learn about new and different stories that you did not know before. You can learn about many more AAPI stories by meeting people in your local communities, looking for books at your library, and more. The Smithsonian can help you on your search for digital resources you can use with a computer or a phone.

VISIT THE *WE ARE HERE* SMITHSONIAN LEARNING LAB COLLECTIONS

The Smithsonian Learning Lab is a digital tool that allows you to explore Smithsonian collections online. We created thirty collections that invite you to explore many of the big ideas and significant moments introduced in this book. These collections expand the stories of each Asian American and Pacific Islander person in the book with images from the Smithsonian's collections as well as websites and archives created by AAPI community organizations across the United States and the Pacific.

Each Learning Lab provides you with opportunities to further unpack the AAPI experiences described in the profiles through the inclusion of additional resources about people and places mentioned in the text. You'll be able to see a photographic portrait of Chien-Shiung Wu, a drawing of Jerry Yang, a magazine cover featuring Keanu Reeves, images of masks worn by Naomi Osaka, video interviews with Shirin Neshat, and much more. These collections will help you understand more about the individuals, their lives, and their communities.

With a phone app or a phone's camera, scan the QR code below to access the *We Are Here* Learning Lab collections. With a personal computer or a computer that you can access at school or a library, you can access the collections by visiting https://learninglab.si.edu/org/apac.

Each *We Are Here* Smithsonian Learning Lab collection includes images of artworks, photographs, archival materials, links to community-created websites, key terms, and guiding questions for discussion or quiet reflection based on the following people:

- Etel Adnan
- Eddie Aikau
- Grace Lee Boggs
- Lydia X. Z. Brown
- Momi Cazimero
- Manny Crisostomo
- Taimane Gardner
- Calvin and Charlene Hoe
- Schuyler Miwon Hong Bailar
- Dinah Jane
- Kathy Jetñil-Kijiner
- Dwayne "The Rock" Johnson
- Channapha Khamvongsa
- John Kneubuhl
- Bruno Mars
- Carissa Moore
- Shirin Neshat
- Amanda Nguyen
- Naomi Osaka
- Craig Santos Perez
- Mau Piailug
- Keanu Reeves
- Lakshmi Singh
- Vishavjit Singh
- Thenmozhi Soundararajan
- Teresia Teaiwa
- Philip Vera Cruz
- Hinaleimoana Kwai Kong Wong-Kalu
- Chien-Shiung Wu
- Jerry Yang

We hope you enjoy learning more about each person through the Smithsonian Learning Lab.

GLOSSARY OF TERMS

The Smithsonian Asian Pacific American Center highlights the stories and experiences of people who are connected to Asia and the Pacific—a geographic region that covers more than one-third of the earth that includes West Asia, North Africa, East Asia, Southeast Asia, South Asia, and the Pacific. This includes the history, culture, and contemporary perspectives of people living in the islands and atolls of the Pacific where they have resided for millennia, before US imperialism, but are presently occupied by the United States, specifically Hawai'i, American Sāmoa, Guåhan/Guam, and the Northern Mariana Islands, as well as the perspectives of sojourners, immigrants, and refugees who came to the United States from countries across the Pacific and Asia.

This glossary provides definitions and explanations for terms present throughout the book. These terms and more are included in the *We Are Here* Smithsonian Learning Lab collections.

Alaia: Small thin surfboard, as of breadfruit or koa wood, and heavier than the olo board (wehewehe.org).

Caste or Caste System: Caste is a system of oppression established in Hindu scripture to determine a person's social status and purity at birth. The four-varna caste system consists of Brahmins (priestly class) at the top, then Kshatriyas (warriors, rulers), then Vaishyas (merchants), and at the bottom Shudras (peasants). Those existing outside of this system, including Dalits and the Indigenous tribal people, also referred to as Adivasi, are on the receiving end of caste apartheid violence (Equality Labs).

CHamoru: Language and people (Guåhan/Guam) | **Chamoru:** Language and people (CNMI): The official name and spelling of the Indigenous inhabitants and language of Guåhan/Guam is "CHamoru" and as "Chamoru" in the Northern Mariana Islands. The word is spelled this way (capital *C*, capital *H*, lowercase *a-m-o-r-u*) when referenced in both English and CHamoru. The spelling of the term is "CHamoru" when referencing people and language of Guåhan/Guam and "Chamoru" when referencing people and language of the Commonwealth of the Northern Mariana Islands (CNMI).

Disability Justice: The cross-disability (sensory, intellectual, mental health/psychiatric, neurodiversity, physical/mobility, learning, and more) framework that values access, self-determination, and an expectation of difference. An expectation of difference means that we expect difference in disability, identity, and culture (Naomi Ortiz, Disability Activist Collective notes, edited 2014).

Gender: Gender refers to socially constructed and enacted roles and behaviors that occur in a historical and cultural context and vary across societies and over time. All individuals act in many ways that fulfill the gender expectations of their society (National Institutes of Health).

Hinduism: A religious, philosophical, and cultural tradition that developed in India with the composition of the Vedas, characterized by belief in a supreme being of many forms and natures, by the view that opposing theories are aspects of one eternal truth, by the desire for liberation from earthly evils, and by belief in reincarnation (thefreedictionary.com).

Hōkūleʻa: A double-hulled voyaging canoe first sailed in 1976 as a pivotal cultural moment during the Hawaiian Renaissance marking a cultural reclamation of Hawaiian knowledge and identity.

Identity: An individual's sense of self, defined by both a set of physical, psychological, and interpersonal characteristics that is not wholly shared with any other person and a range of affiliations (ethnicity) and social roles (American Psychological Association).

Islamophobia: There is not one clear definition of Islamophobia. It is a term that can encompass many negative prejudices and harmful treatment of people who are Muslim or perceived to be Muslim, regardless of whether they are religious. It homogenizes and collectively punishes large groups of people based on prejudices. The prejudice most salient in Islamophobia is the presumption that Muslims are terrorists, have a high risk of becoming terrorists, or are secretly planning or associating with terrorists. This prejudice has wide adverse effects on individuals and communities, from state-sponsored Islamophobia (government surveillance as an example) to private Islamophobia (discrimination against individuals or communities in the workplace and bullying as examples) (Sahar Aziz, Rutgers University).

Kalo: Taro (*Colocasia esculenta*), a kind of aroid cultivated since ancient times for food, spreading widely from the tropics of the Old World. In Hawaiʻi, taro has been the staple from earliest times to the present, and here its culture developed greatly, including more than three hundred forms. All parts of the plant are eaten, its starchy root principally as poi and its leaves as lūʻau (wehewehe.org). Hawaiʻi's cosmogony links the Hawaiian people and the Hawaiian islands to common ancestors, where Kalo is the elder sibling to humans. Kalo therefore holds a sustaining position in the culture as a food source and a vital link to the land and ancestors.

Kuleana: Right and responsibility (wehewehe.org). Kuleana is a uniquely Hawaiian value and practice that is loosely translated to mean "responsibility." The word *kuleana* refers to a reciprocal relationship between the person who is responsible and the thing for which they are responsible (ʻŌlelo Community Media and Hawaiʻi News Now).

Māhū: In a Hawaiian cultural context, a māhū person is a Native Hawaiian person who embodies a third gender. *Māhū* is a Hawaiian word that refers to a third gender that existed in Hawaiian society before continual contact with foreigners and persists in contemporary Hawaiʻi. The word *māhū* is casually used—many would argue misused—to describe transgender or gay identities. In Hawaiian language and culture, māhū is not necessarily synonymous with LGTBQ+, although Native Hawaiians who identify as māhū might also identify with aspects of LGTBQ+ culture and discourse.

ʻŌlelo Hawaiʻi: The Hawaiian language.

Paipo: A short surf board, a body board (wehewehe.org).

Refugee(s): Human beings forcibly displaced within or outside of their land of origin as a result of persecution, conflict, war, conquest, settler/colonialism, militarism, occupation, empire, and environmental and climate-related disasters, regardless of their legal status.

Sikhism: A monotheistic religion founded in northern India in the 1500s by the guru Nanak. Sikhism rejects caste distinctions, idolatry, and asceticism and is characterized by belief in a cycle of reincarnation from which humans can free themselves by living righteous lives as active members of society (thefreedictionary.com).

SWANA: An acronym that stands for South West Asia North Africa.

Transgender: Used to describe someone whose gender identity or expression is not typically associated with the sex assigned at birth. It can be used to describe people with a broad range of identity or expression. Someone who identifies their gender as androgynous, gender queer, nonbinary, gender nonconforming, MTF (male to female), or FTM (female to male) may also consider themselves to be transgender (Gender Equality Law Center).

ʻUkulele: A stringed instrument invented in Hawaiʻi by a Portuguese immigrant from Madeira named Manuel Nunes. Nunes, along with early ʻukulele innovators and fellow Portuguese immigrants Augusto Dias and Jose do Espirito Santo, combined and eliminated aspects of other stringed instruments common in the Madeira and the Azores Archipelagos to create what is now considered the standard design of the ʻukulele.

Acknowledgments

SPECIAL THANKS TO:

Smithsonian Asian Pacific American Center:

Lisa S. Sasaki, Director, Smithsonian Asian Pacific American Center · Theodore S. Gonzalves, Interim Director, Smithsonian Asian Pacific American Center · Healoha Johnston, Curator, Asian Pacific American Women's Cultural History · Andrea Kim Neighbors, Manager of Education Initiatives · Lawrence-Minh Búi Davis, Curator of Asian Pacific American Studies · Kālewa Correa, Curator of Hawaiʻi and the Pacific · Adriel Luis, Curator of Digital & Emerging Media · Nafisa Isa, Program Manager · Marynissa Pedroza, Staff Assistant · Wendy Kennedy, Administrative Officer · Catherine Lee, Senior Advancement Officer · Mary Woodward, Advancement Assistant

Smithsonian Enterprises:

Carol LeBlanc, President · Brigid Ferraro, Vice President, Business Development and Licensing · Jill Corcoran, Director, Licensed Publishing · Kealy Gordon, Product Development Manager